Profiling, recording and observing

2

Profiling, recording and observing
A resource pack for the early years

Teachers' Guide

Barry Stierer, Jane Devereux, Sue Gifford,
Elizabeth Laycock and Janet Yerbury

This *Teachers' Guide* supports the use of two recording notebooks, the *Classroom Observation Notebook* and the *Parent Discussion Record*.

First published 1993
by Routledge
11 New Fetter Lane, London EC4P 4EE

British Library Cataloguing in Publication Data

A catalogue record for this title is available from the British Library.

ISBN 0–415–08964–6 (Teachers' Guide)
    0–415–08965–4 (Notebook Pack)
    0–415–08966–2 (Complete set – Notebook Pack and Teachers' Guide)

Typeset in 11/13pt Optima by J & L Composition Ltd, Filey, North Yorkshire
Printed in England by Clays Ltd., St Ives plc.

Contents

Figures

Background and acknowledgements

This *Teachers' Guide*, and the two recording notebooks which accompany it[1], were produced as part of a research and development project carried out jointly by the London Borough of Merton Education Department and the Faculty of Education at the Roehampton Institute, both in south-west London. The project began in 1989 and was on-going at the time these resources were produced in 1992. The project's objective was to design a set of materials to support profiling, recording and observing in the early years, to pilot those materials in Merton first schools, and to refine the materials in the light of continuing evaluation.

'PROCESS' was the name adopted by the project team. This was the acronym for the project's full title (*P*rofiling, *R*ecording and *O*bserving *C*ompetences and *E*xperiences at the *S*tart of *S*chool). At the same time, 'PROCESS' conveyed the project's commitment to qualitative and formative recording based on teachers' and parents' observations of everyday processes of learning, and its rejection of quantitative measurement of outcomes which reduces the process of learning to numerical scores or ticks in boxes.

Throughout this Guide, we regularly refer to the project and its recording materials using the 'PROCESS' name which was used during the research and development phase.

Although this Guide was written by members of a core project team, the 'PROCESS' project has benefited from contributions by a large number of people during its lifetime, and we should like to acknowledge those contributors and express our thanks for their support and assistance.

First and foremost, we owe a tremendous debt to the headteachers, classroom teachers and nursery nurses in the 32 Merton first schools where the 'PROCESS' material was piloted during 1989–90, 1990–91 and 1991–92. We are especially indebted to those members of staff who fed back to the

[1] This *Teachers' Guide* supports the use of two recording notebooks, the *Classroom Observation Notebook* and the *Parent Discussion Record*, published by Routledge.

central team the evaluations of their efforts to integrate the material into their schools and classrooms. That feedback has played a critical part in the writing of this Guide. Equally, our sincere thanks are due to Merton children and their parents.

During the initial research and development phase of the project, the following individuals formed the 'core' project team:

- Sue Gifford (Roehampton Institute, Faculty of Education)
- Elizabeth Laycock (Roehampton Institute, Faculty of Education)
- Linda Pound (Roehampton Institute, Faculty of Education)
- Leo Rogers (Roehampton Institute, Faculty of Education)
- Jane Salt (London Borough of Merton, Early Years Advisory Teacher)
- Barry Stierer (Roehampton Institute, Faculty of Education) (Project Co-ordinator)

During those early days the project team enjoyed the support, and benefited from the contributions of:

- Lesley Kant (London Borough of Merton, Chief Inspector and Deputy Director of Education)
- Tony Ford (London Borough of Merton, General Inspector [Early Years])
- Harriet Strickland (London Borough of Merton, General Inspector [Special Needs])
- Roy Evans (Roehampton Institute, Faculty of Education)

As the project expanded, the following individuals contributed to the training of teachers and nursery nurses in the use of the 'PROCESS' material; to the school-based support of staff using the material; and to the evaluation and refinement of the material:

- Jane Devereux (Roehampton Institute, Faculty of Education)
- Alison Kelly (Roehampton Institute, Faculty of Education)
- Sandy Peperell (Roehampton Institute, Faculty of Education)
- Sue Smedley (Roehampton Institute, Faculty of Education)
- Anne Washtell (Roehampton Institute, Faculty of Education)
- Maggie Williams (Roehampton Institute, Faculty of Education)
- Janet Yerbury (London Borough of Merton, General Inspector [Early Years])
- Suzanne Gordon (London Borough of Merton, Early Years Advisory Teacher)

The photographs which illustrate the Guide were taken in Merton first schools by Margaret Sargent (Roehampton Institute, Early Childhood Centre).

Finally, the project benefited considerably from the moral support and expert technical advice of our two external consultants, Desmond Nuttall (Department of Educational Research, London School of Economics) and Norman Thomas (former Senior Primary HMI and Emeritus Professor of Education, University of Warwick).

A note about available programmes of training in the use of the material

This *Teachers' Guide* has been produced to support the introduction and use of the 'PROCESS' recording materials in schools and classrooms. Our intention has been to provide a resource which addresses the full range of issues which are likely to be raised by school staff attempting to use the package. We hope that individuals or teams who wish to lead training sessions based on the 'PROCESS' material will find much in this Guide to support them.

In addition to the training which schools and local education authorities may wish to conduct, it may also be possible for members of the 'PROCESS' project team to make a direct contribution to training programmes in local areas. For details, please write to:

The Director of Education and Recreation
London Borough of Merton
Crown House
London Road
Morden
Surrey SM4 5DX

1

Introduction

THE 'PROCESS' PACKAGE

'PROCESS' is a comprehensive package of materials to support observation, recording and reporting in the early years. It has been developed by a team in south-west London, based in the London Borough of Merton and at the Roehampton Institute, and has undergone three years of piloting and evaluation in Merton first schools. 'PROCESS' has been designed principally for use by nursery teachers, nursery nurses and reception class teachers. More information about the project which produced these materials is provided in 'Background and acknowledgements' at the beginning of this Guide.

The 'PROCESS' package supports two vital and related stages in the assessment of young children in the early years: the formative stage and the summative stage. By *formative* we mean the gradual building up of a picture of young children's learning and development, through everyday observation of them engaged in classroom activity and through discussions with parents. We consider formative recording to be a professional task which enhances the effectiveness of teachers' planning and reviewing of their provision for individual children.

By *summative* we mean a kind of 'stock-take' at around the time of the child's fifth birthday, when evidence from the formative stage is summarised and commented upon for wider reporting purposes. A summative record brings together significant information about a child's learning and development at around the time the child begins compulsory schooling, and portrays retrospectively the pattern which has built up over time. It then forms the basis for discussions with parents and for communication with the child's receiving teacher, and serves as an essential qualitative 'baseline' which will enable sensitive interpretation of the child's achievements at the end of Key Stage 1 of the National Curriculum.

The 'PROCESS' package supports the formative stage by providing two specially designed notebooks for everyday use by teachers and nursery nurses: the *Parent Discussion Record* and the *Classroom Observation Notebook*. These twin elements of the formative stage are described in detail later in the Guide, and form the heart of the 'PROCESS' system.

The package supports the summative stage by providing (in Chapter 4 of the Guide) detailed advice on the production of summative records, together with an example of a summative record form used by teachers and nursery nurses involved in piloting and evaluating the package.

The distinctive features of the 'PROCESS' system can be summarised as follows:

- The system is based upon a coherent and clearly articulated view of teaching and learning in the early years, and of the way in which regular observation and recording can support that approach.
- It reflects a model of observation-led recording which is embedded in everyday classroom activity, rather than a model based upon isolated behaviour, checklists or 'performance indicators'.
- It supports the longitudinal and cumulative collection of evidence directly related to individual children's learning and development and spread over a wide range of learning contexts, which enables a deeper understanding of progression through the early years.
- It has a cognitive emphasis, in contrast to some assessment and record systems for the early years which emphasise children's social, emotional and physical development. It also emphasises the importance of children's attitudes to their own learning.
- It places central importance upon a partnership with parents.
- It allows for contributions from a range of adults working with the child, such as nursery nurses, nursery assistants, etc.
- The system is designed explicitly to contribute to the forward planning of classroom activities for individual children, based upon a growing understanding of the child's needs and abilities.
- It contributes directly to the production of a valid and comprehensive 'baseline' at the point of entry to full-time schooling which may enable the evaluation of progress represented by children's National Curriculum assessment results at the end of Key Stage 1.
- It fully acknowledges the importance, relevance and validity of teachers' classroom-based judgements of children's progress, whilst at the same time contributing to the continuing development of teachers' skills of observation and formative assessment.
- It embodies a coherent theory of assessment, recording and reporting which can provide the starting point for whole-school developments of practice and policy.

A NOTE ABOUT THE CONTEXT IN WHICH 'PROCESS' WAS DEVELOPED

It is worth explaining at this stage that the 'PROCESS' system was developed and piloted in 32 first schools in the London Borough of Merton. Merton

LEA has one of the most generous early years provisions in the UK. Virtually all of Merton's first schools have a nursery class or early years unit catering for the under-fives, and the great majority of children in the borough have had the benefit of several terms of nursery experience before they begin school formally at five. This was understandably an essential aspect of our research and development project, since it was possible to develop an early years record which could be built up gradually in the period leading up to the legal point of school entry, rather than one based on a more concentrated 'snapshot' during a child's first few months at school. Nevertheless, we feel that the system is easily adaptable to other circumstances, such as those in which children enter school at the time of – or even after – their fifth birthday. Individual schools and teachers will need to consider how best this adaptation should be made.

HOW THE GUIDE IS ORGANISED

This Guide has been written to be used as a resource rather than as a booklet to be read through once! We have organised it in a way which we hope will enable you to find the sections you need at any time easily and quickly.

In Part One, the two formative recording elements (the *Parent Discussion Record* and the *Classroom Observation Notebook*) are described in Chapters 2 and 3 respectively. These chapters explain the purposes and functions of the two notebooks, and provide detailed practical guidance on their everyday use. Chapter 4 is concerned with the summative stage of the package, and provides advice on the production of summative records as well as practical examples of summative records prepared by teachers and nursery nurses involved in the project.

Whereas Part One is addressed primarily to the classroom practitioner, Part Two is addressed to school managers, INSET providers and advisory staff, and discusses the systems and frameworks of support which are essential to ensure the success of the 'PROCESS' package in schools. Chapter 5 describes the way in which 'PROCESS' was introduced to teachers and nursery nurses taking part in the piloting and evaluation project, and discusses questions which we feel need to be considered when introducing 'PROCESS' in classrooms, schools and LEAs. Chapter 6 describes the regular review and discussion, within and between schools, which were features of the project, as well as the essential role played by headteachers and advisory teachers.

Note: We have used the generic term 'teacher' throughout this Guide to include nursery teachers, nursery nurses, reception teachers and other staff working in nursery schools, nursery classes, infant schools and infant departments of primary schools.

RATIONALE

Our starting point is that children of all backgrounds and abilities bring with them, whenever they start school, a rich and individual collection of knowledge, skills, attitudes and experiences, and that if we are to devise a learning programme for the child starting school which builds directly on 'where the child is' we need to have some kind of systematic and professionally valid way of documenting that wealth of competence and experience.

This argument sounds relatively uncontroversial. However, it is important to acknowledge that it flies in the face of traditional assumptions about young children. Those assumptions are based on the view that some children come to school better able than others to benefit from schooling. According to this traditional view, some children, because of their greater intelligence, or their advantaged background (including opportunities for pre-school education), are 'ready' to benefit from school immediately they start. Others are 'deficient' in one or more respects, and the urgent responsibility for schools is to compensate for that deficiency by trying systematically to bring them up to the state of readiness which their more favoured peers had reached before they started school. The child-centred philosophy, on the other hand, challenges these traditional assumptions because it suggests that *all* children are ready to benefit from school unless they are severely brain-damaged, and that if some children are deemed 'not yet ready' to benefit from school the problem lies with an over-narrow

definition of what schooling comprises rather than with a deficiency in the child. Of course we are all well aware of the dramatic differences between young children. However, according to the child-centred view, these differences are not linear differences between children who are more or less ready to benefit from school, but individual collections of strengths which, if properly documented and understood, enable teachers to support each child in its own existing course of learning and development, rather than effectively to start from scratch.

The body of research evidence supporting this perspective on children's development is now impressive. Language is perhaps the most obvious area in which children bring a stunning degree of expertise with them when they arrive at school. Research carried out by, for example, Gordon Wells and his colleagues at the University of Bristol (Wells, 1986), and by Barbara Tizard and Martin Hughes at the Thomas Coram Research Unit in London (Tizard and Hughes, 1984) demonstrates the sophisticated linguistic knowledge which children have acquired by the age of five. Not only are five-year-olds – virtually without exception – competent users of spoken language for a range of purposes and in a range of contexts, but they also demonstrate a shrewd understanding of the functions served by language and a sensitivity to the subtleties and nuances of meaning in language.

Furthermore, in the area of reading and writing, it is now clear that virtually all children of four-and-a-half or five years have at their command a sophisticated orientation towards print, both in books and in the environment, whether or not they are able to read and write in the formal, technical sense. The rapid growth of research in the area of 'emergent literacy' enables us to build up a picture of the young child in relation to literacy which differs significantly from the one we had only ten years ago (see, for example, Heath, 1984; Teale and Sulzby, 1986; Hall, 1987).

We now know, for example, that young children will, by the time they start school, have spent a lot of time studying literacy-based elements in their environment and observing people using literacy, and that they will have put some powerful intellectual effort into unravelling the phenomena of reading and writing. They will have drawn some perceptive conclusions about literacy. They will understand, for example:

- that reading and writing achieve what might be called 'non-literate ends' – that is, that reading and writing are tools to be used in the pursuit of social and personal communication;
- that we are surrounded by meaningful print – at home, in the environment, on TV, etc.;
- that when we read we rely on the print to carry the message;
- that (whatever the language) we follow the print and turn the pages in a certain order;
- that print is made up of letters, words, punctuation and spaces;
- that there are relationships between the words spoken and the print

observed, but also that the language used in books and other written material is different from the language used when we speak;

- that print is different from pictures; and
- that there is a language associated with the activity of reading books – 'front', 'back', 'page', 'word', 'letter', etc.

These are enormously important aspects of literacy learning – far more important, for example, than the kind of visual discrimination which we used to think children had to master before they were able to learn to read. John Richmond (1988) has said that by four or five years old virtually all children are already using 'all the big gears' in relation to literacy – that is, they know what literacy is for and they know how readers and writers behave. The fact that some children may demonstrate less of an orientation towards books than others should not cause us to assume that they are not equally knowledgeable about literacy.

Similarly, in the area of mathematics, recent research demonstrates that a great deal of important learning takes place before children start school. Martin Hughes's work (1986), for example, shows:

> that children start school with considerable abilities in the area of simple addition and subtraction, provided that the numbers are small. These abilities are most likely to be elicited by clear concrete problems, the meaning of which children can easily grasp.
>
> (Hughes, 1986: 35–6)

Children are also able to count in order to solve practical problems, and 'their counting strategies are frequently untaught' (ibid., p. 36), but arise naturally from their attempts to solve problems confronting them. As with literacy, these findings about children's mathematical ability challenge our conventional understandings of what happens to children when they start school. Hughes argues that if it could be shown

> that children possessed very few abilities on starting school, then perhaps their subsequent difficulty with school mathematics might be easier to accept. Instead, we have something of a paradox: young children appear to start school with more mathematical knowledge than has hitherto been thought.
>
> (ibid., p. 36)

In that case, their difficulty with school maths must have as much to do with our conception of school maths and with our expectations of young children, as with the children themselves.

All these research findings suggest that we should build our early years curriculum on the sophisticated knowledge, skills, attitudes and experience which children bring with them when they start school. If we are going to do this, we have to find ways of finding out and describing that rich background. We need to be sensitive to the full range of knowledge children might bring with them; we need to know where and when to look to discover that knowledge; we need to know how to describe it. In short, we need to develop something like the skills of the anthropologist to uncover the culturally embedded knowledge and meanings which young children possess, and to do so in rich detail and without judgement. A valid early years 'entry profile' ought to help us.

We see the 'PROCESS' system as a practical expression of this rationale in four inter-related ways.

Forward planning

First, the forward planning of activities for individual children can, from their very first day in school, be informed by real insight into their patterns of learning and development, gained through regular structured observation and discussion with parents. As these insights accumulate, this forward planning will progressively build more precisely upon each child's real competences and experience of learning.

Reviewing provision

Second, 'PROCESS' supports teachers' regular reviewing of their provision for individual children, based upon evidence gathered through observation and discussion. If teachers take the time and make the effort to plan their provision for an individual child in a way which reflects an evolving understanding of the knowledge, skills, attitudes and experiences which the child has 'brought to school', it stands to reason that the recording system should enable the teacher to evaluate the effectiveness of that provision, and to use the information gathered through the formative recording process to carry out that essential and continuous review. This may amount to little more than a recognition that the child has not been given adequate opportunities, or guidance, to experience certain activities. Information gathered through regular observation would provide the evidence for such a recognition, and would lead naturally to an effort to modify provision for the child. This is an example of what we refer to elsewhere in this Guide as 'observation-led teaching'.

Identification of a child's strengths and weaknesses

Information collected through observation and discussion may contribute to the identification of patterns in a child's learning and development which become a cause for sustained concern and which require action of a more formal kind and which may involve consultation with others. In this sense the 'PROCESS' package is designed to support the initial stages of identifying children's special educational needs, by providing a focus for reviewing each child's progress in their first phase of schooling and by enabling authentic evidence to be gathered which may feed directly into other forms of diagnosis and assessment.

Summative records

Fourth, the gradual accumulation of evidence relating to the child's patterns of learning and development contributes directly to the preparation of a summative record at around the time of the child's fifth birthday. In this way the formative process of observation and discussion will ultimately feed into the process of summative reporting. A summative record serves two purposes. First, it serves as an 'entry profile', which provides an essential focus for reporting to parents at this crucial transition point in the child's schooling and a vehicle for passing on accumulated insights to the child's receiving teacher and to other interested staff within and outside the school. Second, it serves as a 'qualitative baseline' which will enable teachers to discuss the significance of a child's National Curriculum assessment results at the end of Key Stage 1 in terms of the progress such results represent since the time the child started Key Stage 1 at the age of five. We discuss these summative reporting issues more fully in Chapter 4.

VALUES AND ASSUMPTIONS

In declaring our rationale in the previous section, we are aware that we have based the 'PROCESS' system on certain values about early childhood education, and that we have made some assumptions about the extent to which those values are shared by professionals using the material. We feel that it is vital that we try to make our values and assumptions as explicit as we can. We will have achieved this aim to a certain extent in the course of the discussion in the previous section. However, there are several additional points which we wish to make here, and to which we shall return in later chapters.

'Observation-led teaching'

First, the development of the 'PROCESS' system has been informed by a commitment to a style of working in the early years classroom which might be described as *observation-led*. In this we are placing particular value upon classroom practices where structured observation and recording of children engaged in activity are not only natural and routine parts of the teacher's role, but that the organisation of teaching and learning in the classroom is essentially driven by this vital observation work. There is no doubt that building observation and recording into normal classroom teaching is a challenge. However, observing and recording are not ends in themselves. This kind of practice, which Yetta Goodman has called 'kid-watching', can be enormously rewarding, since it can provide you with insights into

individual children which cannot be gained in any other way, and can enable you to evaluate the suitability and effectiveness of your provision for individual children. It can therefore help you to feel much more professionally effective and 'in control'. Moreover, it is our view that the assessment of young children can only be valid and authentic when it is achieved through the gradual building up of a picture of the child based upon evidence collected over time in a range of everyday contexts. Unless observation and recording can become integral features of everyday teaching and learning, the assessment of young children will in essence be an artificially contrived and one-off 'snapshot' or 'test', where children's records depend upon their performance on a single occasion and in circumstances which both teachers and children find stressful and untypical.

Observation-led teaching requires careful planning if it is to become something routine and automatic rather than something done during the odd moment when an opportunity presents itself. This will suggest a classroom organised around activities which do not require constant teacher supervision, direction and involvement. Examples of such activities are group problem-solving tasks which require children to work and talk collaboratively, block play, role play, sand, water and so on. A classroom divided into workshop areas also facilitates independent activity. It ought to be said that such independent activities are important whether or not one wishes to carry out observations and recording! 'PROCESS' has been most successful in classrooms where this style of working is the explicit aim, and it has helped staff to make significant progress towards achieving observation-led teaching. More advice and examples of such practices are provided in Chapter 3.

Supportive working relationships

Second, we have also made assumptions about the kinds of working relationships within the school (and beyond) which help to form the professional context in which the 'PROCESS' system will operate. We have encouraged the teachers and nursery nurses taking part in the piloting of the 'PROCESS' material to develop support networks in order to share their experiences of using 'PROCESS'. This has taken place within individual schools, where teachers and nursery nurses have introduced 'PROCESS' on a team basis, and kept the scheme under review in a collaborative and supportive way. It has also taken place between schools, through meetings in the local professional development centre, and through visits to schools by members of the project team. We discuss these kinds of supportive frameworks in more detail in Part Two, but it is worth highlighting here at the start of the Guide that, since our system is not merely a recording format but also a focus for positive professional development, it naturally depends upon – and at the same time contributes towards – collaborative working relationships within and between schools.

Partnership with parents

Third, the 'PROCESS' system assumes at the very least a commitment in principle to a genuine working partnership with parents of young children, and an eagerness to draw actively upon the unique knowledge which parents have about their own children as learners. Integral to the 'PROCESS' approach is a programme of discussions with parents which are based on a recognition that parents are children's most significant teachers – especially during the first five years. They therefore have considerable insight into their child's learning and development to which school staff may not have access. These discussions communicate an important message to parents: that we value their role in their children's education, and that the effectiveness of our teaching depends on their active involvement. As we elaborate more fully in Chapter 2, the essential differences between an open-ended 'PROCESS' parent discussion, and an interview for briefing a parent on how best to prepare their child for school, will only be achieved when this commitment to partnership is genuine and heartfelt.

REFERENCES

Hall, N. (1987) *The emergence of literacy*. Sevenoaks: Hodder & Stoughton/UKRA.
Heath, S.B. (1984) *Ways with words: language, life and work in communities and classrooms*. Cambridge: Cambridge University Press.

Hughes, M. (1986) *Children and number: difficulties in learning mathematics*. Oxford: Basil Blackwell.

Richmond, J. (1988) Lecture to conference on 'Writing in the primary school', Roehampton Institute, November.

Teale, W.H. and Sulzby, E. (1986) *Emergent literacy: writing and reading*. Norwood, New Jersey: Ablex.

Tizard, B. and Hughes, M. (1984) *Young children learning: talking and thinking at home and at school*. London: Fontana.

Wells, G. (1986) *The meaning makers: children learning language and using language to learn*. Sevenoaks: Hodder & Stoughton.

Part One

Using the material

2

Using the *Parent Discussion Record*

PARENTS AS PARTNERS[1]

There is now increasing recognition that parents are children's first and most significant teachers, especially in the first few years of life. Parents' insight into their children's learning and development can feed directly into the work of staff in school. The information provided by parents about children's interests, enthusiasms and attitudes as well as about what they know and can do is the foundation on which teachers can build. What teachers know about individual children enables them to plan appropriately and to make provision which will develop children's understanding and support the growth of new concepts and knowledge.

There is also growing appreciation of the value of genuine home–school partnerships: the child's home life, parents and community language have real educational relevance. If, when the child starts school, we are to build on previous experience and really start 'where the child is' we need to find ways of enabling parents to share their insights with us. We also need to let parents know very early in the child's educational life that their knowledge of the child is valuable to us, that the effectiveness of our teaching depends on their active involvement and that we value the contribution they make to the child's educational progress.

The 'PROCESS' *Parent Discussion Record* is designed to provide a supportive framework for discussion with parents and a format for recording and structuring conversations.

HOME–SCHOOL LIAISON

Traditionally, teacher discussion with parents has been something of a one-way process with the school informing the child's family about the school's expectations or about the child's behaviour and progress in school. Staff in

---

[1] The generic term 'parent' is used throughout this book to include all who stand *in loco parentis* – guardians, foster parents, carers (if the child is in care or in a children's home) and so on.

most nursery and reception classes have already developed ways of meeting parents and families before a child starts school, and ways of requesting information.

Some schools use questionnaires which are filled in by parents, with the child, at home. Many arrange home visits when a teacher or nursery nurse may simply meet the child informally or, alternatively, take information and booklets about school to inform both child and parents. Others invite the child and parent to visit the school or nursery before the starting date to give the child a sense of what school is all about and to reassure anxious parents. Some schools add more formal explanatory meetings to such visits.

The discussion with parents developed in the 'PROCESS' project is designed to operate in the *other* direction, with parents informing their child's teacher about the child's life and learning outside school. The 'PROCESS' *Parent Discussion Record* is intended to build on existing practices by providing a format for recording information given by parents in such discussions.

SETTING UP THE PARENT DISCUSSION

On the basis of our experience piloting the 'PROCESS' material, we can offer the following advice and guidelines for setting up discussions with parents, which should help to ensure that they achieve the broad aims described above and generate relevant information for the *Parent Discussion Record.*

- If parents are to feel relaxed about this conversation it is important to make it as informal as possible. A sudden, formal summons to 'come up to the school' may be intimidating for many parents, just as a demand to visit at home may be seen as an invasion of privacy. Wherever possible the invitation to school or the request to visit at home should be made on a personal basis, by word of mouth rather than in writing.
- Effective use of the *Parent Discussion Record* does not depend on home visiting. Some schools may feel that visits to the child's home are more valuable than discussions in school, others will feel the reverse.
- When the discussion takes place in the school setting the venue should be as informal as possible. We have found that where meetings are arranged in a parents' room or even in the staff room the resulting conversations are more genuine, relaxed and informative than ones which are held in the headteacher's study with the teacher ensconced behind the desk. You should try to ensure that there are no interruptions or distractions.
- If the discussion takes place at home it is better if the child in question can be looked after by someone else, if possible away from home, in order to avoid eavesdropping and interruption.
- Discussions should be approached with the intention of having a real conversation rather than an interview with an agenda to be covered. The first few conversations may take half an hour or so, but once you are used to having this type of discussion, you should allow about 20 minutes for each one. When invitations are issued it is worthwhile indicating how long you will have available to talk to individual parents. If, at the end of that time, you feel that there may be more to be said, suggest that another time is arranged when the conversation can be continued, rather than running over into the next appointment time.
- 'PROCESS' discussions are generally most successful when they aim only to serve limited purposes. In particular, discussions which aim to provide opportunities for parents to share with school staff their insights into the child's learning and development are generally more successful if they are not 'overloaded' with other matters. If home visits are undertaken they might be used for the school to pass on information, whilst a 'PROCESS' discussion, held later in the school, would be about the parent's knowledge of the child. Alternatively the home visit could be for the 'PROCESS' discussion and parents would come to the school to receive information. It is important, though, that the two types of conversation are not attempted on the same occasion.

- The way in which you arrange the discussion with parents will convey much about the value you place on it. A willingness to accommodate parents before school or in the evening as well as during the day-time demonstrates the importance you attach to these discussions. Equally, it is important to find out about the family's preferred language, if English is not the first language, and to enable them to use the language of their choice. This may mean inviting parents to include another family member in the discussion, who can act as interpreter. If a member of the school staff shares a language with parents it would be a good idea for that person to arrange and carry out the 'PROCESS' discussion. Where neither of these alternatives is possible you will need to find out what provision is made by your Local Education Authority or your local community group for translation and inter-preting so that you can use their services when the need arises.

- At the beginning of the discussion it will need to be pointed out that this conversation really is so that the teacher can be better informed about the child; the parents are the real experts and we need to know as much as we can find out if we are to provide as well as we can for their children.

- It is important to avoid bombarding parents with a list of closed questions: the aim is to enter into a genuine conversation about the child and to avoid being judgemental about anything that is said. Questions like, 'Does he go to the library?' or 'Can she write her name?' can be intimidating and are likely to produce short answers. Such questions carry an implication that these things should be happening and if they are not the child will compare unfavourably with others. On the other hand, open questions like those in the transcript below can encourage conversation:

Teacher: I wonder if you've ever noticed that he likes a particular toy, or whether he likes to play a particular game?

Mother: Well, sometimes he likes one thing for a day or two. It's often because his big brother gets something out, like the toy garage and all the cars. If he leaves them when he goes out to play then R. will want to play with them and he'll want them for sometimes a week . . . then he'll go on to something else.

Teacher: Does he get very involved when he's playing? Sometimes children get so into a game, they don't even notice if you talk to them!

Mother: It depends what it is he's got out . . . if it's his turtle things you can talk till you're blue in the face and he'll take no notice. He talks to himself when he's playing with them, like he's telling himself a story . . . he makes them talk to each other, in the voices, you know, on the programme. But he's not the same with all the toys.

Teacher: I've seen children who sing to themselves, or hum . . . have you ever noticed that?

Mother: No, not really. He tries to sing songs off the radio a bit, but he doesn't get them right. Oh, I know . . . he used to sing bits of things before he went off to sleep – you know, bits of rhymes from the children's telly.

Teacher: A lot of children seem to like rhymes and songs, don't they? They pick them up from the television and from each other when they're playing, and sometimes they have favourite ones in books and comics. Have you noticed him looking at books or comics or newspapers . . . perhaps you've read something to him . . .?

Mother: His brother will sometimes read a bit of the turtle comics to R., but he doesn't let him get his hands on them! He's got a book of stories and he likes me to read some of them to him, especially when he's a bit tired. And he sits and listens when we read the books from school. He likes looking at the pictures and saying what he can see in them. . . .

- At the end of the discussion you may have found out very little about those aspects of the child which you had had in mind, but a great deal about those aspects of the child which concerned the parent. In many ways this should be seen as a mark of successful management of your own role in the discussion, as the parent(s) would have taken a controlling part in the conversation.

THE ELEMENTS OF THE *PARENT DISCUSSION RECORD*

- The 'PROCESS' *Parent Discussion Record* is a loose-leaf notebook. It is designed so that pages can be put in or taken out easily and so that it can be adapted in any way which suits an individual teacher.
- The covers are rigid so that they can be used to create a firm writing surface.
- In each notebook there is a fold-out flap which can be used as a prompt sheet whilst the record is in use. The flap reminds the user about the three separate parts of the parent discussion and includes a range of possible topics for discussion. When in use the flap extends beyond the edges of the notebook so that it is easy to refer to.
- The notebook is made up largely of blank recording sheets, printed double-sided. On one side, space is provided for rough notes and jottings to be made, either in preparation for the discussion or whilst it is taking place.
- On the reverse side there is space for writing the agreed summary of the conversation when the rough notes have been discussed with the parent.

USING THE *PARENT DISCUSSION RECORD*

The parent discussion is divided into three parts:

- Part one: Introduction and explanation
- Part two: The conversation
- Part three: The summing up

The flap in the recording notebook gives prompts and suggestions for planning and conducting each of these three stages.

Introduction and explanation

The aim of the introduction is simply to set the scene. In an informal, relaxed way try to put parent(s) at ease; explain the purpose of the discussion and the notes that you will be taking.

Below is a sample of points you might make in such an introduction. These are included for guidance only; it is not intended that they should be read out verbatim. You will want to put your welcome and explanation into your own words.

> I'm very grateful to you for giving up the time to see me like this. I know how busy you are. I hope you understand that we feel it's very important to talk to parents about their children, especially at this early stage.
>
> This is an opportunity for you to share with me your knowledge about _____, so that I will be able to build on that knowledge in my work with her/him at school.
>
> Parents are their children's most significant teachers – especially during the first five years of life. It is so important that I find out what you have learned about _____ over the years, since you have been so closely involved with her/his learning up to this point.
>
> I don't have many specific things I want to find out from you about _____. Really I just want to chat informally in order to get a better idea of how you see her/him, and what you have noticed about her/him in different kinds of situations.
>
> The important thing is for you to tell me about _____. There may be things you want to ask me about, and I'll try to answer as best I can, but I hope that you'll do most of the talking and I'll do most of the listening!

Then go on to explain the shape of the discussion.

> I hope that we can have 20 minutes or so of informal chatting. I may make a few notes in my notebook, just to remember the points you make. These aren't private or anything, and I'm quite happy to show them to you.
>
> At the end of our chat I'll go over the points you've made just

to make sure I've understood them properly. At that stage, I may make a few more notes – again, just to help me remember.

If at the end there are things you want to tell me that we haven't talked about, don't hesitate to bring them up.

It is important to reassure parents that nothing will be recorded about them or their child without their knowledge and that all records are open for them to see. Equally you may need to assure them that this record of your conversation will not become a part of any formal record, but will be seen only by you, other nursery staff and themselves. Occasionally, in conversations, sensitive personal matters will arise that you agree not to record.

After the discussion you may want to show parents what has been written, or read it out to them if you think that is more appropriate. Alternatively, when you have completed a summary of the discussion, at a later date, you may like to show parents the record whenever they are in school.

The conversation

The main part of the discussion is called a 'conversation' to highlight the fact that it is not an interview, or even a specified list of points that need to be covered. It should be approached with the aim of giving parents the opportunity to tell you about the aspects of their child's development, learning, behaviour and interests that they think are important.

Perhaps the best way of preparing for the conversation is to think through ways of putting parents at ease, ways of framing genuinely open-ended questions and of intervening as little as possible. Most parents enjoy talking about their children and we have found that, once things get going, there is little difficulty in finding things to talk about. We found that beginning the conversation by asking parents to show us photographs of the child as a baby never failed to break the ice and establish the right atmosphere.

Part of your preparation for this part of the discussion might be to jot down on the record sheet a few 'topics of conversation' you think might be appropriate, drawing on anything you already know about the child or the family. You may find the list of topics on the flap a useful resource: this list is by no means exhaustive and is not intended to be an agenda for the conversation.

During the conversation you can jot down notes on the record sheet to act as an *aide-mémoire* in recalling later the main points a parent makes. Two or three words will probably be enough to remind you.

The summing up

The last part of the discussion is the 'summing up': by referring to the brief notes made during the conversation, you should state the main points the

This page is for jottings and *aides-mémoire*. Two or three words may be
enough to remind you of the point made by the parent. You may also want
to use this page for notes in preparation for the discussion.

- games at home with older sister
- experiences at play group
- story tapes — plays them at home?
- a good dancer?
- block play - patterns (last week)

Figure 2.1   An example of notes taken during a parent discussion.

parents have made. As you do so you can write each point on the reverse
side of the record sheet so that the parent(s) can see what is being written
down. You may prefer to give a verbal summary of the main points at this
stage and then write up the record to show to parents at a later date.

Whichever you choose to do, the list of points need not be rounded statements or even complete sentences. This record is essentially a memo addressed to yourself, though it is important that you share with parents whatever has been recorded.

At the bottom of this side of the record sheet there is a space for 'Further details'. You may find this is a useful space for noting specific factual information which you feel is important to ask about at the end of the discussion, or which the parent volunteers. Topics which might feature here could include health, physical development, care-givers, siblings, specific difficulties such as hearing problems and so on.

TIMING OF PARENT DISCUSSIONS

The *Parent Discussion Record* is not designed exclusively for use before the child begins nursery, or before statutory schooling. Some schools may wish to arrange such discussions with parents before the child begins in school; others may prefer to leave it for a few weeks. Some schools in the pilot study used home visits for meeting the child and informing parents about nursery/school routines, times, expectations and so on before the child began school and then invited parents to an informal discussion in school, for the purpose of completing this record, a couple of weeks after the child started.

Schools that have carried out this kind of discussion with parents when children are in nursery classes may wish to carry out follow-up discussions when children transfer to reception.

Some schools who had used the 'PROCESS' *Parent Discussion Record* in conversations with parents early on in children's schooling have arranged to share with parents a summative record of progress at the end of the school year (see Chapter 4). Such records, which draw on both observation gathered in the 'PROCESS' *Classroom Observation Notebook* and information offered by parents in initial conversations, have been received most enthusiastically and positively. Many have been pleased to find that information they had given to teachers had been noticed and had clearly been of value.

Partnerships created and records begun when children start schooling form a secure foundation for collaboration between home and school, which can be built on as schooling continues. Parents who start by talking with teachers in this way are likely to be willing to return to school for further conversations as their children move through the school.

3

Using the *Classroom Observation Notebook*

The value of observation as part of the teaching and learning process has always been acknowledged. Observation is generally more effective when it is supported by a structured framework. The 'PROCESS' *Classroom Observation Notebook* provides just that, and this chapter of the Guide provides some strategies to help you start and maintain your observations.

This chapter is divided into four main sections:

- Planning for observations
- Using the notebook
- The headings on the flap
- Reviewing observations

We provide a series of questions which highlight many of the issues surrounding the use of the notebook, followed by some solutions that have been used by teachers involved in the project. These are provided for you to select from and use as you develop skills of observing.

PLANNING FOR OBSERVATIONS

ORGANISING THE CLASSROOM

How do you organise the classroom?

In order to feel free to observe children, and to be able to write notes in the middle of a busy classroom, it is essential that the children are as independent as possible. You will need to ensure that they are not coming to you with problems they could sort out themselves. This is desirable in any case, so that your time is spent in quality interaction and evaluation of what is going on, rather than in low level maintenance or merely asking short questions.

The creation of a general attitude of independence takes some time to set up, and you must allow for this. It is even harder if you do not have a core of children who are used to the way the classroom works, and who can set the tone and help others.

These are some of the aspects that teachers have found it useful to consider:

- Are resources readily available for the children? Do the children know where to find things? Do they know where to put them back? The use of pictures, coloured symbols and silhouettes, as well as written labels are ways of encouraging independence.
- Do they know how to use resources? Initially time needs to be spent showing children how to use resources. Keeping to a minimum things requiring adult assistance (like apron-tying) needs some thought.
- Do they know where to put finished products? Setting up a short-term display area for finished products can enable children to see a task right through to the end, including display.
- Do activities and provision stimulate prolonged involvement? Are they rich in possibilities for extension by the children? Equipment that can be combined in different ways, that offer choices, such as large and small construction toys, more than one role-play area, and basic resources being easily accessible to children, all help children to develop independence and their abilities to extend and expand activities for themselves.
- How can you encourage self-reliance? Many children need encouragement to take responsibility for their own learning and managing resources for themselves. Encouraging them to be independent and confident takes time, but your observations can help you to monitor this.

The questions listed below highlight some of the areas and issues that you may need to consider in order for children to gain understanding of expected behaviour and to develop problem-solving skills for themselves.

- Do children know what they might do with the resources available?
- Do children know how to share resources, ask for things, negotiate turn-taking?
- Do they know some strategies to try when they are stuck with something?
- Do they ask each other for help or volunteer help to others?
- Do they know that they are expected to solve problems?
- Do the children know how they might resolve problems themselves?
- Are they confident in problem-solving?
- Do they try alternative strategies?

Children will need help in all of this, and knowing what kind of behaviour is expected of them in different areas. You may need to spend time encouraging them to be more self-reliant by:

- encouraging them to extend play situations;
- posing open-ended problems in the home corner (or other role-play areas) and directing them towards resources to help them solve the problem;
- introducing different kinds of writing they might do;
- modelling how they might share a book; or
- teaching them how to play games.

Adults or other children with the necessary expertise can provide the necessary interaction and intervention to help children over difficulties. Posing problems in role-play areas allows children to go beyond their normal limits as they take on roles and bring their outside knowledge to bear in solving problems. Allowing time for children to talk to each other about how they coped with various situations not only extends their language skills but helps them to reflect on the strategies that they have used to reach their respective outcomes. This encourages creativity and also helps them to develop confidence to take risks and try out their ideas. In looking closely at your provision in this way you begin to see many ways of answering the above questions and freeing yourself to observe.

How can you stop interruptions?

Children can be 'trained' to not disturb you at times you signal: they will come to appreciate that they will get a similarly intensive share of your attention at another time. One teacher even found it useful to wear a 'Do not disturb' hat!

How can other adults help?

You might use other adults such as parents, other teachers and nursery nurses as general helpers or as people with particular expertise to do some of the following:

- to take care of incidental queries, freeing you to observe or work with a group;
- to teach children to use an area, or resources, so that they will be self-reliant in future; or
- to provide expertise in particular areas.

PLANNING YOUR TIME

When do you observe?

Finding time to do observations has to be part of the planning process and the following questions may help you to consider the best times and way forward for you.

Are there some times of the day when you could snatch a few minutes to jot down observations?

By examining the pattern of the day it might be possible to find some slots that could be used to do observations. During outdoor play, story time and tidying up are possible starting places.

Can you observe while working and interacting with groups of children?

Observing does not have to be silent: it can involve talking to children about what they are thinking or doing. You could identify two children of the group you are working with as the ones you are going to make notes on. The notes could be made as you work or immediately afterwards. Children are usually very interested in what and why you are writing and this offers great potential for encouraging early writing!

Can you use other adults to help you?

If you are fortunate enough to have another adult available, you might arrange times when one of you takes care of incidental queries, and the other concentrates on observing. Some people have an understanding that they can ask each other to take over if they want to observe something particularly interesting. One teacher made a point of giving the notebook to any visitors to the classroom (like the headteacher) and inviting them to make some entries while in the room.

TARGETING

There are two main ways of making observations: first, you can note down things that are interesting and significant as and when you notice them. These incidental observations can be the most valuable kind. Secondly, you can plan to make observations, either by identifying a particular child, a particular area or activity, or a time of day. Planning observations in this way we refer to as 'targeting'. Targeting helps you to be systematic in observing all the children, to prioritise your attention, or to collect information which answers identified questions about the way children are using resources, helping you to evaluate these at the same time as monitoring children's development.

Setting achievable and realistic targets is an important way of getting started and maintaining observations. If you leave observing to chance, or when you have the time, you may well find that other things take up your time! If, on the other hand, you try and do too much, you will find that other aspects of your teaching suffer, or that you cannot manage and then feel tempted to give up altogether. If you work as a team of adults in the classroom, then the chances of achieving targets are better if the targets are set collectively.

What are realistic goals/targets?

Below is a list of some ways teachers have set targets:

How many?

- Targeting one child per session/day.
  If several adults work together they may identify a different individual each or they may all do the same one. The respective advantages are covering more children, or benefiting from combined wisdom. Some teachers like to encourage visitors to the room to add their observations of the child identified for the session.
- Targeting a set number of children per week or half term.
  This allows for some flexibility in falling behind and catching up on goals set.

Who?

- Targeting a group of children, such as those who have newly arrived, those giving cause for concern, those about to change class.
- Targeting a group of children with whom you have planned to work.
- Some people prefer to simply work through the register.

In any case, you need to check that you are spending time observing all the children (see section on 'reviewing' below).

Where?

●   Targeting an area of the classroom, or an activity, rather than children. This allows you to evaluate your provision, at the same time as collecting information on individuals. Alternatively, you may target a curriculum area, such as design and technology.
●   Targeting a specific child in a specific area, like outdoors, perhaps because you have particular concerns.

When?

●   Setting a time of day to observe.
    If there are two of you, you could agree that one attends to minor incidents during that time.

How long for?

●   A planned observation of 5 minutes can be very fruitful, but equally . . .
●   Short sightings can be equally revealing, if you are able to ascertain the context.
●   Some teachers have found it useful to look at a child every 10 minutes, and see what they are doing, for a brief moment.
●   If a child is busy in an area near you for 20 minutes, you may be able to record developments over that period.

All these kinds of observations are useful. In any case, it is helpful to build the setting of targets into your planning time, recording the children you are going to observe, where and when you are going to do it. It is useful to use a review sheet (discussed in 'reviewing' below) so that you monitor who you have observed, and whether you are keeping up with your targets. Ticking a sheet, meeting once a week to discuss observations with colleagues, or arranging regular meetings with a co-ordinator, deputy head or an early years cluster group, all help to provide a support structure to keep you on target.

What if you do not meet targets?

If you do not meet targets it is important not to feel guilty or give up: teaching is a very busy job, and there are times when only Superteacher could keep it all running smoothly and find time to record observations as well. Many teachers find it useful to have fallback strategies for when they have not made any observations in a day (or two!):

●   simply put the identified children's names at the top of tomorrow's list;
●   do some observations while supervising outdoor play; or

- jot down a few very quick observations as the children are tidying up, or as soon as they have gone out of the room.

PROMOTING INVESTIGATING AND PROBLEM-SOLVING IN THE CLASSROOM

Young children tend automatically to investigate the properties of anything around them, whether these are physical objects, language or adult behaviour. Investigation in the classroom is likely to arise when:

- materials can be arranged and combined in a lot of different ways (such as blocks, containers, boxes and shapes);
- materials provided have interesting features, which prompt further observation and investigation (such as natural and living things); and
- actions have interesting and surprising effects, which prompt investigation and explanation (for example mixing substances to produce a change of state, as in cooking, or exploring forces which produce sound or motion, as when shaking things, or rolling objects down slopes).

Suitable activities might be construction, cooking, gardening, making objects like hats, setting the table, sharing food, solving puzzles, number games with hidden objects, sorting and tidying. Traditionally, some of these activities, like cooking, are more about following instructions and commenting on what is happening than on investigating, problem-solving and thinking. This is obviously because one is concerned that the product should come out 'right', for example in the case of cooking, one wants the result to be edible! Nevertheless, many simple activities call for discussion of alternative methods, prediction, observation and comparison of materials and effects, and speculation on possible explanations. It is worth encouraging other adults who work with you (if you are lucky enough to have any!) to ask the children questions like:

- What do you think will happen if . . .?
- How could we find out?
- What else could we try?
- What do you notice?
- What else do you notice?
- Why do you think that is?

It is important to emphasise that all children's responses need to be accepted and valued, rather than directly corrected, if the children are genuinely to think for themselves, with confidence, rather than try and guess what the adult wants them to say.

Problem-solving opportunities

We all solve problems all the time, but it can be useful to think how to encourage and develop this, to promote collaborative skills and to enable us to observe how children are putting their knowledge and competences into action.

Problems can arise from different sources, such as:

- a story, e.g. the three bears needing new beds;
- real life, e.g. laying the table or a cupboard that needs tidying up;
- a role-play area with flexible resources for making and rearranging, e.g. things for a shop that needs organising;
- an event, e.g. a party requiring food and hats; or
- flexible materials that can be combined, to prompt the child to devise their own problem, e.g. construction material, or cars and sand.

Problems can usually be solved by several methods, and have more than one solution. Children can be encouraged to be resourceful and flexible if:

- there is a choice of resources to use in solving the problem;
- they are encouraged to think about different methods, and to consider improvements; or
- they are supported at critical moments, e.g. 'This is a bit tricky, isn't it?' or 'I wonder what else we could do?'

USING THE NOTEBOOK

THE ELEMENTS OF THE NOTEBOOK

The *Classroom Observation Notebook* is designed to be practical and flexible, for use in a variety of busy classroom situations by a variety of teachers with different styles of working. It is:

- loose-leaf, to allow recording sheets to be added and taken out easily;
- A5 size, so it can be carried around and used easily;
- supplied with rigid covers that can be folded back, so that it can be used in the lap, or when standing, out of doors, etc.; and
- supplied with recording sheets which are only faintly ruled, so that they can be used as plain or ruled, as preferred.

The main feature of the *Classroom Observation Notebook* is a folded flap with headings and prompts printed on both sides, so that it can be easily referred to by folding it out. These headings provide a framework for analysing observations.

ORGANISING THE NOTEBOOK

Teachers have adopted different strategies for doing this.

How do you organise the recording sheets?

- Name up sheets, one for each individual in alphabetical order, keeping a section of unnamed pages at the back.
- Divide the notebook into sections for each child. If you initially keep all the observations for a child together, you will be able to refer back and monitor developments over the space of a half term or so. Then you can file observations away, or select some to file.
- Make sections for groups of children, such as those most recently arrived or those about to go to another class.
- Name up the sheets for children who you have decided to observe for that day or week.
- If you make notes on several children on the same sheet, photocopy this, and file in sections for individuals.
- Add a review sheet (see 'reviewing' below).

Where do you keep the book?

The observation notebook can be kept on one table so that all adults have access. Other alternatives include having:

- two or three books placed at strategic points around the room;
- clipboards around the room on which the flap has been stuck and several recording sheets clipped to it with a pen or pencil firmly attached;
- pads of recording sheets around the room; or
- a folder or board to collect the day's or week's observations prior to filing.

MAKING ENTRIES IN THE NOTEBOOK

How much should you write?

The length of entry varies considerably from person to person and from observation to observation, but the recurring point made by teachers in the pilots was that it isn't the length that matters, but much more what you write and whether you can read it later! You will find that as time goes on, it becomes easier to pick out the significant behaviour or phrase, and to leave out the less relevant detail. As one teacher put it, 'I find that as time goes on, I write less, but it tells me more.'

DATE, NAME, TIME AND OCCASION	Kylie 30.1.92 Colour mixing red/yellow Asked if order makes a difference
INTERACTION	
ATTITUDES	20 mins
INVESTIGATING/ PROBLEM-SOLVING	
COMMUNICATING, REPRESENTING AND INTERPRETING	Whichever way you do it, it's still orange!
INDIVIDUAL NEEDS/ S.E.N. COMMENTARY	

Figure 3.1 An example of a notebook entry. Note the detail recorded under 'DATE, NAME, TIME AND OCCASION', the note about how long the child persevered at the activity (20 minutes) and the short snippet of overheard talk.

What should you write?

It is important to set any observation in context, and that means you need to put in a date, time and setting. This not only gives you a timing but also serves as a memory jogger when you try to recall the observation for other purposes, e.g. report writing. Use key words, or snippets of conversation that would recall incidents for you.

How should you write?

It is important to write what you saw or heard and not put any interpretations or judgements into the observations. This is easier said than done in some circumstances because as teachers we are continually making assessments as we plan provision. However, the essence of the observation notebook is to build up a picture of the child. Only when we have a number of cameos/vignettes/snapshots can we begin to look for patterns and make judgements. As all records in school are now open records it is important to be sure that these are observations and not value-judgements. Care also needs to be taken about availability of records and storage when not in use.

When should you write?

There are two main ways of making observations: one is to plan a time to observe a specific child (see 'targeting' above) and the other way is to note spontaneously observations when you see something interesting happening. Of course these two methods overlap, and it is important to plan and be systematic. Unplanned observations are, nevertheless, very valuable, and it is better to have several short entries of this kind than infrequent lengthy ones.

USING THE FLAP

The main headings on the extendable portion of the flap ('INTERACTION', 'ATTITUDES', 'INVESTIGATING/PROBLEM-SOLVING' and 'COMMUNICATING, REPRESENTING AND INTERPRETING') suggest things to look for when observing a child, whilst the main body of the flap contains prompts and examples of behaviour to match the headings. Fuller versions of these prompts and descriptions are given below (see 'The headings on the flap').

USING THE COLUMNS AND BOXES ON THE RECORDING SHEETS

The lines on the recording sheets are deliberately faint and broken, so that you can write across them.

The two columns are useful if you want to:

24 Feb, 2pm
Construction

Jason and Dipti

Group making long "treasure line" incl. J.
O. has bricks they want
J. asks D. for bricks

D. refuses
J: we will let you find the treasure
if you give us your bricks.

D. gives bricks, excited
I'm gonna find the treasure!
J. takes bricks, completes lines.
no more interaction with D.
D: you said you'd let me find the
treasure!
J. no response.

Figure 3.2 An example of an entry which simply records a conversation between two children, an example of 'spontaneous observation'.

Amy   9/11
10
– 10·15
making mask

(DATE, NAME, TIME AND OCCASION)

w. Martin
Asking lots of qs.

(INTERACTION)

Swayed between
confidence and can't do
– gives to M.

(ATTITUDES)

Who's small enough to
get their face thro'
here?
You need to cut out
the eyes because
you'd bump into things.
You'd bump into
yourself. You couldn't
see.

(INVESTIGATING/ PROBLEM-SOLVING)

(COMMUNICATING, REPRESENTING AND INTERPRETING)

Cutting skills – not very
sure about which bit
to cut off. Cut off
strips – progressed nearer
to cutting line.

(INDIVIDUAL NEEDS/ S.E.N COMMENTARY)

Figure 3.3 A notebook entry which is strongly structured by the headings on the flap and which includes evidence in each box ('boxing').

- make observations on the same child on different days using the same sheet (you can get four such observations on one page, which is useful for short observations);
- make separate notes on two children, engaged in the same activity. The page may then be photocopied, or cut in half, for filing; or
- write description on the left-hand side and comments on the right-hand side (alternatively you can use the 'INDIVIDUAL NEEDS' box for commentary of this kind.

Alternatively, you can ignore the columns and write across the page.

There are two main approaches to using the boxes – sometimes referred to as 'boxing' and 'not boxing'! Boxing means writing in the boxes next to the relevant heading. This approach particularly suits the quick noting of something interesting which may well be just the child's spoken words and the context. Many people find that writing in the boxes is difficult to start with, but as they become used to thinking in terms of the headings it becomes easier. You will also find that it becomes easier to pick out the significant behaviour, or phrase, and to leave out the less relevant detail.

The important thing is to get something written down, and not to worry too much about getting the 'right' box. If afterwards you think the entry was relevant to another heading, you can still cross-reference, by writing a comment or drawing arrows.

The advantage of writing in the boxes is that you can scan through a child's notes and see a developing profile in a particular area, such as 'INTERACTION' or 'PROBLEM-SOLVING'. And equally, you can scan through and see which aspects you are not writing much about: for instance, that most of your observations for a child are about 'INVESTIGATING', with not much about 'INTERACTION' (see 'Reviewing observations' below).

Not boxing means ignoring the divisions on the pages. Sometimes you may find an observation does not fit in the box: for instance, a long observation of solitary problem-solving, recording a variety of strategies, would need to take the whole page, but would relate mainly to 'INVESTIGATING/ PROBLEM-SOLVING'.

Teachers have devised various methods of relating 'unboxed' observations to the headings. For example, some have numbered the flap headings (e.g. 'INTERACTION' – 1; 'ATTITUDES' – 2, etc.) and then used these numbers against significant parts of the entry. Other teachers have used a system of coloured highlighter pens ('INTERACTION' – pink; 'ATTITUDES' – green, etc.) and coloured appropriate parts of the entry.

You should not feel that you must relate every heading to one observation. It is likely that, for instance, a short, unplanned observation will only relate to two headings. For a child playing with cars on her own, you may just want to comment on 'ATTITUDES' and 'INVESTIGATING'. For children reading together, you may just want to use 'INTERACTION' and 'COMMUNICATION'. Or you may wish to relate the observation to just one

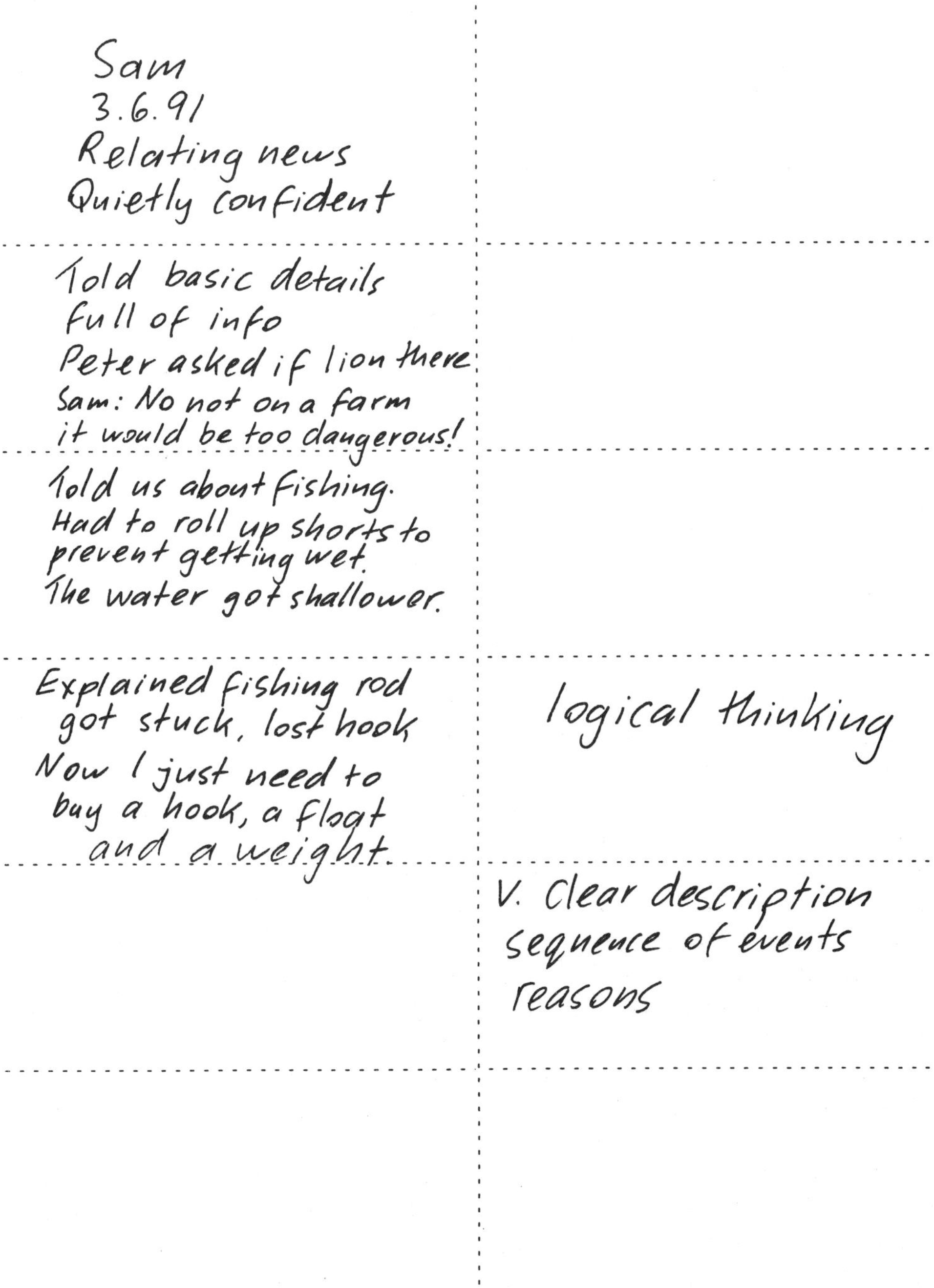

Sam
3.6.91
Relating news
Quietly confident

Told basic details
full of info
Peter asked if lion there
Sam: No not on a farm
it would be too dangerous!

Told us about fishing.
Had to roll up shorts to
prevent getting wet.
The water got shallower.

Explained fishing rod
got stuck, lost hook
Now I just need to
buy a hook, a float
and a weight

logical thinking

V. Clear description
sequence of events
reasons

Figure 3.4 A notebook entry in which evidence is recorded according to the teacher's own priorities at the time ('not boxing').

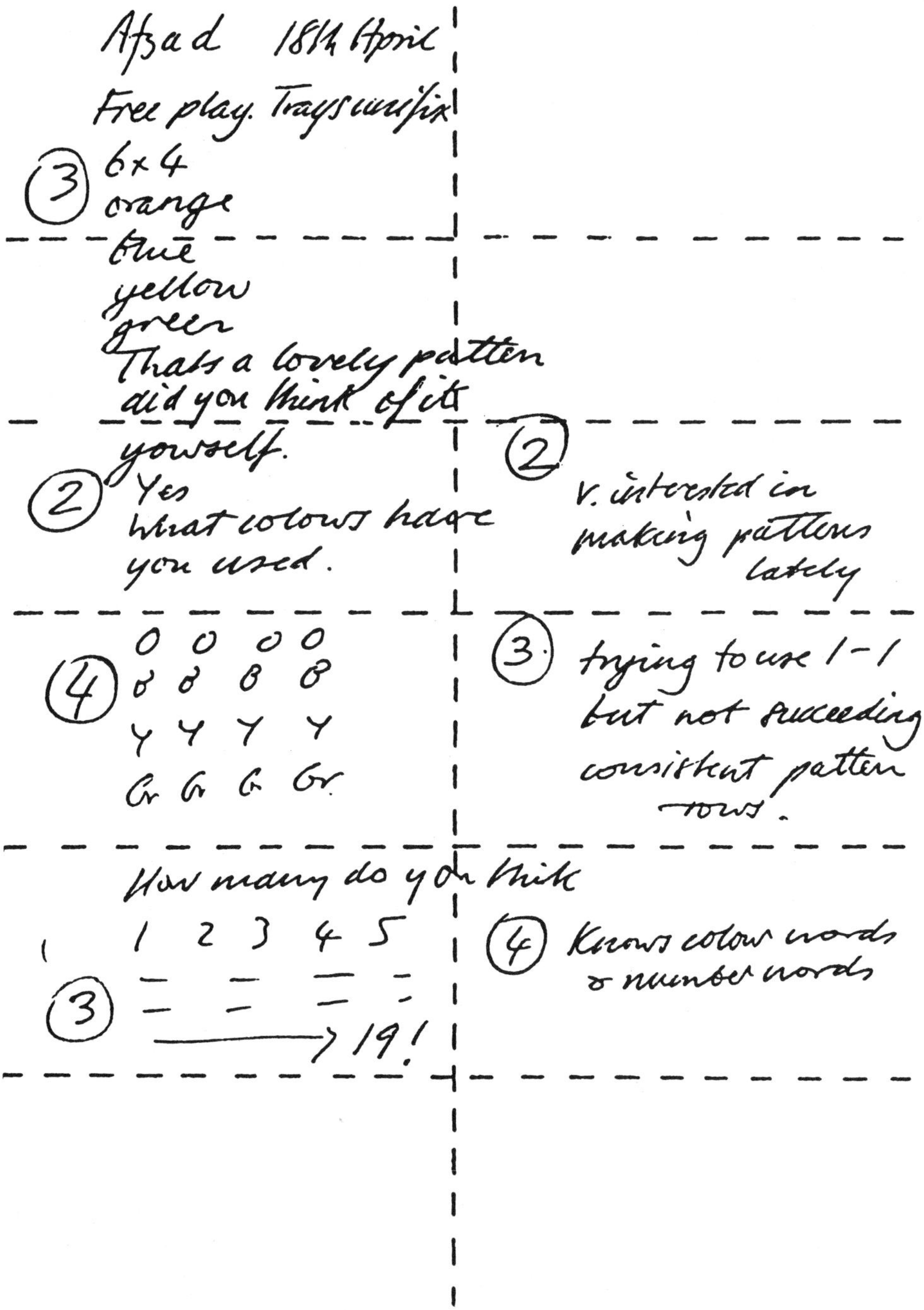

Ajzad   18¼ April
Free play. Trays wwifix
③ 6 x 4
orange
blue
yellow
green
That's a lovely pattern
did you think of it
yourself.
② Yes
what colours have
you used.

② v. interested in
making patterns
lately

④ 0 0 0 0
δ δ δ δ
Y Y Y Y
Gr Gr Gr Gr.

③ trying to use 1-1
but not succeeding
consistent pattern
rows.

How many do you think
1 2 3 4 5
③ = = = = =
——————→ 19!

④ Knows colour words
& number words

Key: 2 = Attitudes
3 = Investigating/problem-solving
4 = Communicating, representing and interpreting

Figure 3.5 An example of an unstructured entry which the teacher has later coded by numbers to relate to flap headings.

particular heading because of your current concerns, for instance if a child's behaviour shows a striking change in terms of co-operation, you may just want to note this against 'INTERACTION'.

On the other hand, a single phrase, used by a child (such as 'two mouses') could reveal thinking processes as well as social and communicating skills. There is no one correct interpretation of a young child's behaviour, and two people will see one action differently. For instance, two teachers noted a boy painting who was trying to copy the pattern of his jumper. One teacher recorded this as 'REPRESENTATION', and the other as 'patterning' (under the 'INVESTIGATING' heading). It might equally have been recorded under 'ATTITUDES', if it marked a pronounced interest in patterns. All these interpretations are valid, and worth considering, as they lead to different decisions about what to provide next for the child. For instance, the teacher might decide to provide opportunities for making representations from direct observation, or for copying and creating patterns in a variety of media, or for spotting patterns in the environment. Alternatively, the teacher might provide all three, and watch to see which the child was more interested in. In fact it is probably better to make several tentative interpretations than categorically to state the significance of a child's actions, which we cannot know for certain. This is the benefit of sharing observations with colleagues.

THE HEADINGS ON THE FLAP

The categories on the flap provide a framework for analysing observations: most aspects of children's significant behaviour will be covered by these headings. This section is organised so that prompts and explanations derived from the headings on the flap are presented in the left-hand column, and practical examples and illustrations of recorded evidence are presented in the right-hand column.

INTERACTION

This heading tends to overlap with 'COMMUNICATION'. It is a question of emphasis: is it the social role of the child that interests you, or the quality of the language used? Noting observations by this heading allows you to monitor the kind of social relationships a child is engaged in, which are important for the child's educational development. Can they learn from and with others, can they learn on their own? These are key questions concerning children's development as learners.

The social context

Who is the child with?

one other child
a group of children
an adult
or is the child alone?

What is the child's role?

giving instructions to everyone
being a 'baby'

What is the adult's role?

teacher directing activity

Social behaviour related to the context

Is the behaviour appropriate or
not?

turn-taking
listening
sharing resources
hitting

Range of social skills

Is the child paying attention to
others?

asking questions and listening to
    answers

Is the child collaborating?

offering suggestions or resources

Is the child able to negotiate for what they want?

maintaining rights
deflecting aggression

ATTITUDES

This section allows you to keep a record of the child's interests and to check whether they have positive attitudes to learning, for you to build on (or else try to do something about). It can be just as important to monitor whether the child has positive attitudes towards learning, as to monitor the learning itself. After all, a child who loves books and feels confident about reading, is likely to learn to read, but a child who has learned to read and hates reading is unlikely to continue to develop as a reader. Similarly, curiosity towards scientific things and processes, or a confidence in solving puzzles and problems, are likely to bode well for children's scientific and mathematical learning.

It is obviously very difficult to read people's emotions from the outward signs of their behaviour (as shy people who have been considered stand-offish know only too well). When recording attitudes, it is particularly important to describe the behaviour you are observing, and to be tentative in attaching emotional significance to it. For instance, staying at an activity for a long time may indicate a nervousness about going elsewhere, rather than involvement, but this may not be immediately apparent.

Response to the context

Does the child behave differently in this area?

behaving confidently only in the home corner?
being aggressive only with the bikes?

Dispositions and interests

Does the child have particular interests?

building with curved blocks
bats
dressing up
dolls and babies
birthday cards and age badges

These can be built on by present and future teachers in order to develop relationships and learning. They may be short- or long-term, relating to particular home circumstances, and very common, but significant for that individual. Aversions or dislikes are equally worth noting, so that you can monitor

them, and decide whether you
should do something about them.

Curiosity and persistence

asking questions
touching, smelling
repeatedly reminding the teacher
   about a promised activity
spending half an hour trying to
   build a bridge.
not wanting to paint
hesitance about joining in a game

INVESTIGATING/PROBLEM SOLVING

Observations against this heading are concerned with finding evidence of
how the children are thinking and what they are learning. This is difficult to
do, but since children learn not only by watching and listening, but also by
testing out their own theories of how things behave, and how rules operate,
it is important to observe them investigating, questioning and reasoning
logically. And since we can only tell if people have really learned something
if they can apply it in a new situation, it is important to see if children make
connections between different contexts, and can actually use their skills and
understanding to solve a problem.
   This heading will overlap with 'COMMUNICATING, REPRESENTING AND

INTERPRETING', because it may be through talking, making models or role-playing that the child shows evidence of problem-solving and investigating.

Investigating: seeing what would happen if . . .

It is hard to identify when a child is investigating a theory, because this investigation may appear as pointless, repetitive and silent action. Sometimes, however, this 'playing around' with materials appears focused, systematic and reflective but, as always, it is important to describe the *behaviour*, in case one is 'reading' too much into it.

mixing water with the sand
pouring a lot of water on the water wheel
mixing blue and yellow paint
printing these shapes together in this way
fitting these things here
arranging these colours in this way
putting large blocks on top of little ones
rolling a cone down a slope

Predicting

Prediction is important, because it requires past experience to be brought to bear upon a new situation, and may prompt or reveal the formulation of a theory (as to how certain things behave when they are heated, for example).

Cooking
mixing flour and water
heating the mixture
freezing the orange juice

Gardening
planting the seeds
not watering them
burying paper, tin, bread

Many activities can be made to involve more thinking if the children are asked to predict what will happen next.

Hat-making
putting this length strip of paper round your head
rolling up this shape of paper
folding, cutting like this, and unfolding

Occasionally it is possible to observe children making predictions, through their actions. You can infer a prediction in what children choose to use, or the method they employ, which presumably they predict will work. Sometimes this is because they have predicted wrongly, and are attempting the impossible, as for instance when the block is far too big to balance on the tower!

Prediction is not just about science and maths; it can be about stories and people.

How will this story continue?
How will a friend feel when their new baby arrives?

Estimating is a particular kind of prediction to do with quantifying, which can reveal understanding.

How many cakes do you think we will be able to make from this mixture?
How many glasses of lemonade do you think we will get out of this bottle?
How many seeds do you think there are in this packet?
How much do you think we should charge for the sweets?
How long a strip do you need to go round your head?

It is also possible to observe children estimating, through their actions.

choosing a container to fill up the baby's bath
selecting a block to fit in a gap
choosing a piece of material to cover the bear's bed

Problem-solving: choosing appropriate methods, materials and tools for a purpose

As is evident from the above examples, it is easier to observe children thinking about solving problems if they are encouraged to choose their own methods and strategies, and are offered a range of materials and tools to choose from. This is not to say that at times children should not be shown efficient ways of doing things, or told how to use tools. Children may also need to be reminded of strategies that they know about, but do not connect to a new situation. However, it is important to monitor how confident children are in tackling problems, and to see whether they can relate experiences from one context to another.

Using strategies

Does the child use a range of alternative strategies, or give up if the first one does not work?

trying a jigsaw piece several ways, rather than hammering it in and abandoning it

Does the child behave systematically?

trying to find the biggest hat, and putting to one side the hats that have already been tried

Does the child divide a problem into sub-problems?

when ordering rings on a stick, reversing the order of just a few, rather than taking them all off and starting again

Does the child, when making things, go through sensible design processes, in terms of planning ahead, checking as they go along, reviewing the finished product, and making improvements in accordance with the purpose?

making a box for a toy out of Lego or Clixi, getting the pieces together first, checking the length while building, making adjustments, then deciding to add a lid

Choosing methods

laying a table by using one to one matching, or by counting the number of places, then the plates

tidying plates in the café, by stacking them in order of size

Choosing materials and tools

making a model or construction, and choosing things which are of appropriate textures, properties, size, etc.

deciding to fix with glue rather than Sellotape

choosing a fine paintbrush for a detailed painting

Children may show through discussion that they know what some sophisticated tools are used for, without knowing how they work.

when discussing measuring, making a ruler by putting lines and numbers on a stick

knowing scales are to do with how heavy you are

consulting a calendar while playing travel agents

telling about mum using a calculator for the catalogue

knowing a thermometer is to do with hot and cold

Children may select appropriate forms for writing and communicating in a certain situation (alternatively, you might note this as 'COMMUNICATING').

lists, letters
maps and diagrams
telephone list

Making, using and articulating their own rules

When children can be observed keeping to a rule this is important to note, because it shows that they are thinking logically. This can be more noticeable when the rule is the child's own.

referring to 'sheeps', reveals a rule that the plural requires an 's'

Organising, sorting and classifying

When a child sorts things consistently according to identifiable criteria, this also shows that she is applying a rule logically, about what goes with what, and why.

tidying up the crockery and cutlery in the home corner

toys and games

deciding on a way of setting things out on the counter of a shop, or putting groceries away in a cupboard, or sorting the books in the home corner

playing with small toys, buttons, beans, shells, fabrics, and arranging and sorting them into groups according to their own criteria (shiny ones over here, a line of red cars and a line of yellow ones)

Making and spotting patterns

This is also about using rules: repeating patterns usually consist of a unit (a motif or small group of shapes) arranged according to an identifiable rule. The rule might be to repeat the sequence ABC ABC ABC, or to reflect it, ABC CBA. Other rules for patterns might be about increasing or decreasing, leading to numerical patterns like doubling. The unit of the pattern might be relatively simple, as with bead-threading, or very complex as with some block constructions.

bead-threading (red, blue, red, blue . . .)

Children may copy and continue patterns, or reproduce them in different media.

copying a knitted pattern with paint

recreating a printed pattern sequence with coloured bricks

working with a partner in a movement session

Children may create their own repeating patterns.	painting, sewing, printing or sticking patterns, to decorate hats, bags, cards or cakes
Children may just notice patterns by looking at them.	commenting on bricks, floors, fences, wallpaper, wrapping paper
They may point out similarities.	'You've got stripes on your shirt like my jumper' 'It's the same but the other way round'
Children often notice and create patterns with words and sentence structures.	noticing rhymes like, 'riddle, tiddle, middle' using the pattern of a story by retelling it, using a repeating structure, but with their own words

Generalising, and making links between one context and another

Examples of this may include examples of things that children appear to know, such as names of colours, numbers, animals and shapes. What is interesting here is not just that they know the word, but the range of contexts that they can apply it to, and the connections they make between them. It is one thing to know where your nose is, but can you spot the nose of a dog, an elephant or a bird? What kind of generalised idea of the form and function of a nose does the child have? Can they relate the word to a network of wider knowledge, or do they just respond with the word on the cue of a teacher pointing to an object? Generalising is part of classifying and pattern-spotting, and is about abstracting an idea or relationship from a variety of contexts and examples.	recognising four counters arranged in different ways recognising different shaped triangles in different positions as being triangles recognising an E on its side, in upper and lower case, in different scripts recognising a range of different reds (including pillar box red, maroon and smoky red) as being distinct from pink or purple saying things like, 'Your badge is the same as the clock'

COMMUNICATING, REPRESENTING AND INTERPRETING

This is about the range and degree of sophistication of skills that a child employs. It can be important, if a child does not seem to be communicating verbally, to see if they are communicating in other ways through gesture and facial expressions, for example. If a child is not representing by drawing, they may be doing so through other media, whole body movement, or dramatic play.

Talking and listening

> justifying a point of view to another
> acknowledging another's viewpoint
> talking on the telephone and using
>   appropriate language
> talking for puppets or dolls

Writing and reading

> using a notebook to write an
>   observation of children playing!
> using a clipboard to make notes on
>   patients in the clinic
> dictating a story, whose
>   composition shows an awareness
>   of story structure
> behaving like a writer, using 'joined
>   up' writing

telling a story from a book to another child

reading and approximating to the text, using one to one correspondence of spoken and written words

using cues from the context or initial letter sounds

developing personal codes, such as drawing stars to represent 'clapping'

Using numerals, tallies, fingers

It is important to recognise children's early efforts with symbols, which might be a series of marks, one for each object.

You may notice a child representing a number with fingers, which is a basic way of abstracting the number from a situation.

holding up three fingers and complaining, 'He's got that many cars and he won't give me any of them'

Drawing and painting

Children's drawings often speak for themselves in terms of what children are concerned to represent, and the choice of colours, textures and techniques they have employed to do so. They may reveal the sophistication of what they notice about people and things. Sometimes it is the process rather than the product which is most significant, especially if a child has used one sheet of paper to paint a succession of 'action' paintings, with a verbal commentary, ending with a thick green wash over the whole piece of paper! For instance, one child painted a fireworks picture with a lot of suitable colours, actions and noises, which involved some sophisticated representations, but one could not have guessed this from the finished product which was several layers of paint thick.

Dance, mime and gesture

Frequently young children use whole body movements very effectively to express themselves or to describe how things move. This might be spontaneous or as part of a dance session. Sometimes the gesture is of equal importance to other forms of communication which it accompanies.

waving hands above head to show how the big horns are of the monster being drawn

Role play, imaginative play and storying

Some children reveal a great deal of knowledge, observation and imagination through role play. Sometimes they are more articulate when 'in role' than in other situations, or show other qualities, of creativity, originality, logical thought, assertiveness or areas of experience, which would otherwise be unsuspected. It is very important therefore to spend time in role-play areas, observing supporting and extending children's play.

Do children use materials creatively to represent other objects?

using a wooden brick as a microphone
using a calculator as a telephone

This may reflect observation of key features and similarities. The provision of 'unstructured' materials, such as boxes, bricks or lengths of cloth, may prompt children to use objects in this imaginative representational way.

Do children pretend that there are non-existent objects, characters and events?

pretending to eat imaginary food
explaining how they got their
    injury in the clinic

This requires even more creativity and imagination.

Do children reproduce or create complex stories in extended play sequences?

acting out the three bears story,
    directing characters as to roles,
    actions and speech

Construction models

Some children show creativity and awareness of similarities of shapes, through using blocks to make representations of buildings, animals and birds. Usually this involves discrimination of curved and straight shapes, similar angles, and so on.

making a 2D representation of an
    elephant using circular and
    elliptical curves appropriately for
    the body and trunk, and straight
    shapes for the legs and tusks
having been shown a fan-tailed
    dove, making one from large
    hollow blocks, using triangular
    shapes together to create the
    vertical fan-shaped tail

Maps, plans and diagrams

Young children may also show some awareness of other kinds of graphical representation.

drawing maps to show visitors the
    way to the headteacher's room or
    the nursery
making a model using boxes or
    bricks to show the layout of the
    three bears' house
doing a drawing of a block
    construction, then referring to it
    later to remake it

INDIVIDUAL NEEDS/S.E.N. COMMENTARY

The final heading on the flap has a different function from the four main headings and requires a special explanation. The four main headings provide a structure for describing what you observe in the classroom. In this final space you can make a brief comment about the evidence you have recorded. Whereas the foregoing notes will be purely descriptive of the child's behaviour you have observed, here you can note the significance of the behaviour, highlight concerns and in effect write a memo to yourself about action to take.

(DATE, NAME, TIME AND OCCASION)	Thomas Running round whole nursery area. 10.5.91 1.45
(INTERACTION)	Playing on his own.
(ATTITUDES)	disturbs other children's play as he goes past – doesn't seem to notice their protests.
(INVESTIGATING/ PROBLEM-SOLVING)	
(COMMUNICATING, REPRESENTING AND INTERPRETING)	pretending to be an aeroplane making loud noises. Didn't respond to me until I touched his arm and looked at him full-face.
(INDIVIDUAL NEEDS/ S.E.N COMMENTARY)	Was he so involved in his own play – or does he have a hearing loss? Nearly always shouts to himself as he plays.

Figure 3.6 Entries showing several teachers' approaches to using the 'INDIVIDUAL NEEDS/ S.E.N. COMMENTARY' heading.

Thomas story time 19.6.91 2.45	(DATE, NAME, TIME AND OCCASION)
small group of children	(INTERACTION)
Thomas chose book about a plane — seemed interested; smiling	(ATTITUDES)
pushed his way to front of group to sit right in front of book, but walked away ½ way through story.	(INVESTIGATING/ PROBLEM-SOLVING)
Shouted "plane, plane", and pointed to pictures but did not comment on story.	(COMMUNICATING, REPRESENTING AND INTERPRETING)
don't think Thomas can hear me — Mum agrees. Book hearing test.	(INDIVIDUAL NEEDS/ S.E.N COMMENTARY)

(DATE, NAME, TIME AND OCCASION)	Sam Start of Nursery session 3.6.91 1pm
(INTERACTION)	Mum leaving nursery. S. holding her legs, shouting and kicking.
(ATTITUDES)	angry, upset, crying took 30 mins to settle.
(INVESTIGATING/ PROBLEM-SOLVING)	
(COMMUNICATING, REPRESENTING AND INTERPRETING)	
(INDIVIDUAL NEEDS/ S.E.N COMMENTARY)	This happens every day since brother born. Talk to mum again - suggest coming later? coming without baby?

	Sankari
	In home corner
	7.5.91.
	10.15am
	playing on her own – dressing up in new sequinned scarves, shawls etc
	smiling happy and confident.
	humming to herself – said clearly to me "I'm going to the Temple."
	First words in nursery after 2 weeks. Must provide more play to link with home – talk to mum. (NB Hindu)

Significance of the observation

The observation may be significant in terms of the child's development: it may mark a new kind of behaviour, or be typical of the child at the moment.

Concerns about the child

Concerns might be about any aspect of the child's behaviour (physical, social, emotional or cognitive). You may want to record a tentative worry, and write a message to yourself to look out for similar behaviour in future.

Action to be taken

In a busy classroom it is helpful to write down reminders to yourself to follow up concerns, rather than try to keep everything in your head. You might want to speak to the parent, another teacher, a dinner assistant, headteacher or other professional, or consult previous records.

You could make a note to try another strategy, encourage the child to participate more in certain activities, or make some extra provision for the child.

You can also use this section to note children's particular competences, for instance, that they know a lot about a particular subject, such as birds, or babies.

And sometimes you will use this box to write down things which, at that moment, do not seem to fit anywhere else.

REVIEWING OBSERVATIONS

STORING SHEETS FROM THE NOTEBOOK

What should you do with your completed sheets?

As observations accumulate it is necessary to think about ways of collecting and storing these. Some teachers have divided the notebook into sections for individuals or groups of children. Others have transferred their sheets to a ring-binder into which they slip samples of children's work, or into the child's individual folder. Initially some schools stored the sheets in a folder or on a general noticeboard in a corner of the classroom out of the physical reach of the children. Later they could be filed away, after discussion of the contents at the end of the day or at a weekly meeting.

TAKING STOCK OF OBSERVATIONS

What, when and how to review?

As the observations accumulate, it is important to look at the range of these in several ways.

What?

- Are targets being met or not: are all the children being covered?
- Are the observations confined to specific children, areas (such as outdoors, or the sand) or aspects (such as interaction)?
- Is the information meeting your needs in terms of monitoring developments, or should you refocus your attention in some way?

When?

Checking at regular intervals helps to make the process of observing into an integral part of your day. Initially it may be important to review how many you have done at fairly frequent intervals to remind you of the task and to help observation become second nature. Time intervals of a week, at the end of a settling-in period, half-termly, termly, or even half-yearly have all been used by different schools.

How?

- A review chart is useful. It could list areas of the classroom so that you can see whether you are observing across your provision.
- A chart listing children ensures that all children are included. If this is combined with the areas, then from your observations it is possible to determine gaps for each individual.
- A chart that lists areas of the flap and children helps to build a picture of the kind of interests and skills that each child is developing as well as identifying gaps. You may discover that you have not seen a particular child investigating or hypothesising, for example.
- For those who work in a team, regular meetings at weekly, half-termly or termly intervals will help to ensure a broad and balanced range of observations. For those who work alone, it is useful to arrange a meeting with a member of the management team, to support you in reviewing.

Why?

Regular reviews will help you to:

- target children, areas or aspects for future observations;
- plan future provision so that you can observe children investigating or hypothesing, for instance;

Talk												
Science												
Outdoor Physical Play												
Music Dance & Drama												
Home Corner & Role Play												
Books & Reading												
Jigsaws												
Drawing & Writing												
Manipulative Activities												
Construction Toys												
Blocks												
Miniature Layouts												
Collage												
Painting & Printing												
Dough Plasticene Clay												
Water												
Sand												
Names												

Figure 3.7 An example of a pro-forma for a cumulative class record of observation entries, highlighting topics and areas for classroom activity.

'PROCESS' CUMULATIVE CLASS RECORD OF OBSERVATION ENTRIES

Child's name	INVESTIGATING	COMMUNICATING, REPRESENTING & INTERPRETING	INTERACTION	ATTITUDES
	Dates and contexts of entries	Dates and contexts of entries	Dates and contexts of entries	Dates and contexts of entries

Figure 3.8   An example of a pro-forma for a cumulative class record of observation entries, highlighting the four main headings on the flap.

- change provision to provide for individual needs both in the short term and the long term; and
- change provision to make it easier to free people to observe.

This section has attempted not only to provide you with starting points for observing in the classroom but also to provide you with a diagnostic tool to identify possible stumbling blocks when the observation schedule is not going as well as anticipated. However, remember that every observation made can only serve to enhance your own skills at observing and develop a more comprehensive picture of the child based on evidence from the classroom. So do persevere and the rewards will be great!

4

Using 'PROCESS' for reporting purposes

RATIONALE

In Chapter 1, we explained that 'PROCESS' supports the preparation of a summative record at around the time of the child's fifth birthday. We mentioned that this summative record can serve two purposes. First, it serves as an 'entry profile' which describes the patterns of the child's learning and development as they begin Key Stage 1 of the National Curriculum, drawing directly upon evidence collected gradually through classroom observation and discussion with parents. Such an 'entry profile' provides an essential focus for reporting to parents at this crucial transition point in the child's schooling, as well as a vehicle for passing on accumulated insights to the child's receiving teacher and to other interested staff within and outside the school. Second, it serves as a 'qualitative baseline' which will enable teachers to discuss the significance of a child's National Curriculum assessment results at the end of Key Stage 1 in terms of the progress such results represent since the time the child started Key Stage 1 at the age of five.

In view of the widespread interest in 'baseline assessment' we ought to explain why the kinds of summative records we discuss in the 'PROCESS' Guide are descriptive and qualitative rather than numerical and quantitative. In particular, we wish to explain why we call the 'PROCESS' summative record a 'baseline' and yet have not advocated the use of National Curriculum levels of attainment, since it is true that a descriptive and qualitative baseline at five is technically more difficult to relate to assessment results at the end of Key Stage 1.

Many teachers are asking what sense it will be possible to make of National Curriculum assessment results at the end of Key Stage 1 (that is, around seven years old), expressed in terms of levels on the 10-level TGAT (Task Group on Assessment and Testing) scale, unless we are able to measure the net progress which those scores represent. In other words, whether we are talking about an individual seven-year-old, or a whole cohort of seven-year-olds, what meaning does, say, a Level 2 attainment have without some notion of the starting point two years previously? If we could establish a baseline at five years old, the argument goes, we could use the results at seven to determine the educational 'value' which had been 'added' to that child or to that cohort of children rather than merely compare them with a national standard.

Such concerns are perfectly understandable, and in one sense reflect the widely recognised principle that net progress is a more valid index of effectiveness than absolute progress. Indeed in our own research and development project one of our objectives was to use the 'PROCESS' material to establish some kind of baseline at five. Nevertheless, we observed with considerable alarm the growing tendency in some primary schools to use National Curriculum levels of attainment as the main 'units of measurement' in their 'baseline profiles' of rising-fives. A number of the profiles we examined at the early stages of our project consisted of little more than records of which Level 1 statements of attainment children were (and were not) able to satisfy at the time of their fifth birthday. Indeed some schools had gone so far as to invent a Level 0 to describe those children who had not yet 'achieved' Level 1 in certain attainment targets at the time they started school.

We took the view that a baseline at five, expressed in terms of levels of attainment on the TGAT scale, would be wrong. Levels of attainment were, after all, never envisaged as ways of describing five-year-olds. When TGAT published its framework for National Curriculum assessment (DES/WO, 1988), levels were seen as possible outcomes of a pupil's National Curriculum assessment at the *end* of key stages within specific attainment targets. In other words, levels were seen as ways of representing retrospectively the point a child had reached at the end of a sustained period of schooling.

Confusion arose when TGAT 'speculated' that 'average' seven-year-olds would reach Level 2 in most attainment targets, and that a level would represent about two years of 'educational growth'. Working backwards, it would therefore appear reasonable to expect most average five-year-olds to be capable of satisfying Level 1 statements of attainment. Such a conclusion would, however, be fallacious. To use Level 1 as some kind of target for rising-fives is a technically flawed and entirely inappropriate application of the concept of levels of attainment, which were meant to represent out-comes of assessments at the end of key stages. It may be true to say that those children who reach Level 2 or Level 3 or indeed Level 4 at the age of seven will have passed through Level 1 on their way to that outcome. It would nevertheless have been largely unhelpful – if not impossible – to have known the precise moment when that happened, and in particular whether it was before or after they turned five.

It is especially unfortunate that the National Curriculum Council, in its publication *A framework for the primary curriculum* (NCC, 1989), per-petuated this faulty reasoning by specifying those Level 1 statements of attainment which they felt most under-fives could be expected to satisfy. Whilst these statements of attainment, as statements, may in theory serve as ways in which the abilities of rising-fives can be described, they take on a pernicious significance when branded as 'Level 1 statements'.

We also took the view within our project that the pressure to establish a quantitative baseline at five arose in part from the Secretary of State's decision in June 1988 (DES, 1988) to reject TGAT's recommendation that there should be no requirement for schools to publish results at seven. The fact that schools are now encouraged to do so has led inexorably to a widespread panic about assessment at five, thus perpetuating the existing downward spiral of assessment. The goalposts may have been moved, but, in relation to the 'PROCESS' project, we felt strongly that this should not force us to carry out inappropriate assessments of children at five.

We decided, therefore, to try to establish a qualitative baseline at five, based on description rooted in observation and discussion with parents, so that the quality of an individual child's progress at the end of Key Stage 1 could be discussed with parents and others. We do not wish to under-estimate the technical and professional skills needed in order to relate such qualitative descriptions to the outcomes of National Curriculum assessment results at seven, expressed as they will be in radically different terms. Whilst we accept that such assessments will not provide the kind of baseline which will enable a linear measure of progress, we feel that assessments of five-year-olds which are qualitative will be technically and educationally valid. We also anticipate that headteachers will find that such descriptive records can be used to summarise certain aspects of the school's intake in order to gauge the school's effectiveness in the context of assessment results at seven. But our overriding principle was that to relate young children's competences and experience at the start of school to numerical levels of attainment on the TGAT scale would be damaging to children, misleading to parents, and would result in an impoverished educational experience for children in the early years.

PRINCIPLES AND PRACTICE OF PRODUCING SUMMATIVE RECORDS

Teachers involved in the piloting of the 'PROCESS' system completed summative records for the children in their classes, using a pro-forma and accompanying guidelines produced by the project team. However, it emerged from the piloting exercise that many schools preferred to develop their own summative records, often adapting the project team's pro-forma. As a result, we have decided not to prescribe the specific approach we piloted, or to provide multiple copies of the pro-forma, as part of the published package. Instead, we have reproduced in this chapter the pro-forma and guidelines we offered to the schools that piloted the materials, and suggest that you may find it useful to use them as starting points as you embark upon your first round of summative recording.

Under each heading below, we reproduce the advice we gave to schools. This is then followed, within most sections, by a 'commentary box' which reports on the experience and feedback of teachers involved in the pilot relating to the issues in that section.

Purpose

The purpose of the 'PROCESS' summative record is to bring forward significant information, accumulated gradually through the 'PROCESS' *Classroom Observation Notebook* and *Parent Discussion Record*, to a concise report which can form the basis for discussion with parents and school colleagues and which can become part of a child's permanent school record. It is intended that the summative record will usually be prepared at around the time of the child's fifth birthday – that is, at around the time the child moves from nursery to reception class, or begins full-time school.

The need for a summative record arises because the 'formative' elements of the 'PROCESS' system are not suitable for the more public reporting purposes identified above. Entries in the 'PROCESS' *Classroom Observation Notebook*, for example, tend to be made hurriedly and in an abbreviated form and are addressed essentially to oneself. Such short entries, frequently made, will only gradually produce a pattern – a picture of the child's learning and development. The summative record tries to draw out that pattern for the benefit of parents, colleagues and others.

Most conventional summative records tend to be filled in 'cold', 'off the top of the head', or they require some kind of special assessment activity to be carried out at the time the record is completed. Rarely do they draw directly upon continuous observations made by the staff during the period they have taught the child. Such summative records might be relatively quick and easy to complete, but have limited validity and fall short of giving a true picture of children to people who do not know them. The 'PROCESS' summative record, on the other hand, is based on the principle that the starting point in preparing such a report must be the information contained in the formative notebooks which are at the heart of the 'PROCESS' recording system. Otherwise, there is no real relationship between the formative process of observation and recording and the summative reporting stage.

The 'PROCESS' summative record is therefore thought of as a stock-taking exercise, a way of portraying retrospectively the pattern which has built up over time. It is firmly rooted in the evidence collected through the formative process. Accordingly, the more regularly detailed entries have been made in the *Classroom Observation Notebook*, the more informative and valid the summative record will be.

The 'PROCESS' summative record sheet

The summative record sheet used in the pilot project was a single sheet of A3, folded to produce an A4 booklet. This is reproduced for information and possible adaptation on the following page.

Profiling
Recording
Observing
Competences and
Experience at the
Start of
School

A research and
development project
sponsored jointly by
Merton LEA and
Roehampton Institute
of Higher Education

P.R.O.C.E.S.S.   SUMMATIVE RECORD SHEET

To be completed at around the child's fifth birthday.
A convenient occasion might be the start of full-time
schooling, or the transfer from nursery class to reception
class.

Child's name _____

Date of birth _____

Date completed _____

Number of terms in school: _____ p/t   _____ f/t

> This record summarises important aspects of the child's
> learning and development in the period leading up to the formal
> start of full-time school. Inside this booklet are a few
> everyday observations of the child made by school staff over
> the past few months, as well as some comments about the child
> which relate to those observations. On the back page there is
> additional information of a more general kind.

Completed by _____

Drawing on contributions from _____

Name of school _____

Figure 4.1 The summative record pro-forma used during the piloting phase of the
'PROCESS' project.

———— SELECTED OBSERVATIONS ————

1

Date of observation _____ Age of child _____

2

Date of observation _____ Age of child _____

3

Date of observation _____ Age of child _____

COMMENTARY	NEXT STEPS
Interaction	
Attitudes	
Investigating/problem-solving	
Communicating, representing & interpreting	
Individual approaches/needs	

ADDITIONAL INFORMATION
languages spoken/understood, physical development (gross/fine), special knowledge and interests, individual needs

Commentary	Next steps

Parent contribution/comment

- The front cover of the booklet contains spaces for very basic factual information about the child – name, date of birth, etc.
- The two facing pages on the inside of the booklet comprise the central record. On the left-hand side is space for up to three 'observations' taken from the *Classroom Observation Notebook* and edited for presentation in the summative record.
- On the right-hand side is space for general commentary on the child which relates directly to the evidence presented on the facing page.
- On the back cover is space for additional information – that is, information you wish to include about the child but which does not arise from the evidence presented on page 2 – as well as for parental contribution and comment.

Selecting entries

Your aim on page 2 of the record sheet is to bring forward from the 'PROCESS' *Classroom Observation Record* two or three 'observations' which will, in turn, provide the evidence upon which more general commentary will be made on the facing page.

The process of selection should begin by reading through all the entries in the notebook about the child. Some entries may now strike you as superficial, whilst others may seem to capture aspects of the child's learning and development in a particularly telling way. It is unlikely that you will have made entries which capture the precise moment when learning of an especially significant kind happened for the child, or when the child changed in some other way. It is also unlikely that a single entry will somehow 'typify' the child. The most useful entries to bring forward are therefore those which you feel are important to pass on to receiving teachers, other colleagues and parents.

Some entries may seem to be unintelligible to anyone but yourself. These entries may nevertheless be worth selecting and editing for the summative record. It is crucial that you choose entries which capture what you feel are important aspects of the child's learning and development, rather than those which seem to you to be the fullest or clearest.

Ideally you should select entries for the summative record which, taken together, reflect the full range of headings on the flap in the *Classroom Observation Notebook*, rather than just one or two. It would be unrealistic to expect the entries to provide an absolutely comprehensive picture of the child. No record can do this. Records which purport to record every aspect of a child's learning and development only do so by generalising and by being superficial. Your records will be more valid because they will describe certain aspects of the child more vividly and in detail.

Generally speaking, recent entries are likely to be more appropriate and informative than entries made some time ago. This is not necessarily the case. Each observation will be dated on the record sheet, and there will be an opportunity on page 3 to comment on previous stages of learning and development (for very recent observations) or subsequent stages of learning and development (for earlier observations).

Commentary

In the pilot we found that teachers need time to experiment with this area but with practice the process of selection becomes easier. Some teachers initially had difficulty 'trusting' only two or three observations to offer sufficient information about the child. Others had trouble deciding what significant information the observations were offering about the child's achievements and progress. The criterion common to all was the need to reflect a picture of the whole child. In general, the following criteria were considered:

- observations taken at different ages of the child which reflect development at significant points of progress;
- a selection of observations in a variety of contexts which reflect the overall development of the child; and
- positive observations reflecting what the child can do/achieve.

Some teachers were still at the stage of feeling that they needed to incorporate aspects of previous recording systems in the 'INDIVIDUAL APPROACHES/NEEDS' box of the summative record, but were realising that as they developed confidence in 'PROCESS' and their own observational skills such systems were becoming redundant.

Editing entries and managing the summative record

Having selected your entries, you may feel that they are sufficiently 'telling' in their raw state and can simply be copied out on to the summative record sheet. If so, fine!

On the other hand you may now wish to edit them, since at the time they were made the entries probably only had significance for you. The idea now is to turn them into 'stories' which will be readable and useful to others.

The examples you carry forward to the summative record are rather like the stories we tell each other about children every day. They are quite often funny, and are always rooted in a real time and place. It is important that they are therefore dated and tell the story of what you observed the child doing at a particular time and in a particular place. The entry you have chosen may only be three or four words which now jog your memory of the event you observed at the time. In such cases you may have to search your memory banks to fill in the details of the event. If so, try to be accurate and detailed in the way you extend the notebook entry.

Commentary

We found that where there was more than one teacher working with the children it was important for them to set aside time to discuss in detail the accumulated observations in order to present a clear picture of the child. In the main, the responsibility for the writing has been undertaken by the teachers, but schools may like to consider this as a task shared with nursery nurses. Teachers have found that with experience the total time for the task of writing one summative record decreases. One school adopted the system of anticipating the number to be written before a cohort of children transferred, and set themselves the target of discussing and writing one each day. All the nursery staff discussed the choice of observations, the commentary was written at the time and then the observations and the additional information sections were completed later that day by the teacher. Some teachers are considering the use of the summative record at an interim stage (i.e. before the fifth birthday) to offer a stock-take of observations to date. In this way they might reduce the burden of writing all their records at the point of transfer.

Using the 'Commentary' (page 3 of the record sheet)

Generally speaking this section provides you with an opportunity to explain why you have selected the observations which appear on page 2. By picking out aspects of the observations for comment under the five headings you will be helping to answer such questions as:

- What is the significance of the selected observations?
- What do the observations convey about what the child understands, can do, and pays attention to?
- Is the child's behaviour as described in the observations 'typical' of the child's behaviour generally? Does the child usually do this in this kind of situation?

The five headings are intended to help structure your comments. The most important principle here is that your comments on page 3 must arise from the selected observations on page 2 and only from those observations. You should avoid making generalised statements about the child which are not directly related to the observations. Although this may convey a partial view of the child, what you do present will be valid, since it arises directly from observed activity. Remember that there will be an opportunity to make more decontextualised comments on the back page of the record sheet.

You may, in these comments, want to refer explicitly to one or more of the observations on page 2. For example:

'The first observation opposite shows how much more attentive Christopher is to patterns and shapes than he was when he started nursery. He can classify toys, buttons etc. into sets, but is always watching others to see if he is right.'

On the right-hand side of page 3 is a column labelled 'Next steps'. This provides the opportunity to convey to the receiving teacher the strategies you would adopt if you were to teach the child for a further period of time, structured by the headings. You may want to indicate here, for example, what in your opinion the child's particular needs are, in a particular area of her or his learning and development. In this way you are providing a degree of progression and continuity from one stage of the child's schooling to another.

Commentary

In our practice we found that information had been passed to the receiving teachers about the individual children through meetings with the nursery teacher and the nursery nurse which had been set aside for this purpose. In this way the 'Next steps' part of the record was communicated orally and then agreed in written form by both teachers. This enabled the receiving teacher to feel a part of the next stage of planning for the child's development. In other situations the teacher from the nursery wrote the 'Next steps', which were then conveyed to the receiving teacher both through the record and orally.

Perhaps the most important aspect of conveying the 'Next steps' is that the information is conveyed dynamically before the child transfers and is acted upon by the receiving teacher. The traditional model of the receiving teacher forming his/her judgements about the child prior to reading the records can no longer be considered appropriate practice: for effective maintenance of progression and continuity in children's learning it is vital that teachers trust and act upon the professional judgement of their colleagues.

Use of the 'Additional information' section (page 4 of the record sheet)

On the back page of the record sheet is space for additional information which you wish to include about the child but which does not arise directly from the 'observations' presented on page 2. You may, for example, wish to comment on:

- any languages other than English which the child speaks or understands;
- aspects of the child's physical development which constitute a note-worthy achievement or a cause for concern;

- particular interests, activities or hobbies you are aware of, or areas where the child has demonstrated particular knowledge; or
- any aspects of the child's behaviour or learning which have not been described in an 'observation' but which you feel are important to draw to the the attention of parents and colleagues (for instance, an early indication of Special Educational Need).

Like page 3 of the record sheet, this section also has a column for 'Next steps'. This is an opportunity for you to indicate to a receiving teacher the strategies you would adopt, arising from the points you have made in this section, if you were to teach the child for a further period of time.

COMMUNICATING THE SUMMATIVE RECORD TO PARENTS

The final section on the back page of the record sheet ('Parent contribution/ comment') can be used flexibly. You may wish to enter in this space information recorded in the 'PROCESS' *Parent Discussion Record* which you feel is important to pass on but which you have not observed directly yourself.

Alternatively, it is hoped that the summative record will provide the focus for discussions between staff and parents and this space may be useful for recording the points arising from such discussions. You may therefore wish to use the space to record the comments made by the child's parent about the information in the summative record, or invite the child's parent to enter their comments themselves.

Commentary

We found that the summative record has been well received by parents. Their greatest pleasure has been in the recognition of their child through the observations. Many have commented, 'That's just like my child' or 'I can just see her doing that'. Parents have felt clearly encouraged that their child has been valued by the teachers and have been appreciative of the time and trouble given to the records and their child.

Most schools used it as the basis of a parent conference at the point of entry to main school from the nursery. We found that parents were invited to visit school for about 20 or 30 minutes to share the record in a conversation with the teacher. In general, these conversations enabled the teachers to elaborate on information about the child, and the parents to ask questions. Parents were invited to make written comments about the child in the appropriate box in the record and to sign the record, thereby formalising their participation in the process.

One school has adopted the procedure of inviting the parents to talk to each other in a separate room before writing comments on the record.

Whilst we have no figures to confirm this, it seems that about half of the parents chose to add comments themselves while the other half preferred to add a signature only. In other cases the parents asked the teacher to append their views. In another school the record was sent to parents inviting them to respond on a separate comment form, to be returned to the school and then transferred to the summative record. In all cases parents kept a copy of the record for themselves and in a number of schools it has been adopted as an annual report to parents.

THE SUMMATIVE RECORD AND KEY STAGE 1 ASSESSMENT

So far, we have discussed the value of the summative record as an 'entry profile' at the start of formal schooling. At this point we offer some advice as to how the summative record can be used in conjunction with National Curriculum assessment at the end of Key Stage 1 – that is, at around the child's seventh birthday. We have already explained, in the introduction to this chapter, why we decided to reject the use of National Curriculum levels of attainment as an assessment 'currency' for rising fives. Nevertheless, we fully recognise the importance of discussing with parents the progress represented by their child's end-of-Key Stage 1 results, and we strongly encourage users of the 'PROCESS' package to use their summative records for this purpose.

We provide below examples of the links between the headings on the summative record and the results of National Curriculum assessment. You will note that we present this information through the 'PROCESS' headings, which emphasises the importance of discussing the whole child rather than merely attainment targets. We also take the opportunity to draw attention to the inter-relationship between the attainment targets.

Interaction

This can be considered particularly in relation to English AT1 (Speaking and Listening), and also to AT3 (Writing). In AT1 children 'discuss their work with other pupils and the teacher', they plan activities collaboratively, they engage in collaborative play, and they 'participate as speakers and listeners in a group engaged in a given task'. In AT3 children should be encouraged to 'write in groups, sharing their writing with others and discussing what they have written'. Information on children's achievement in these areas at the end of Key Stage 1 can be related back to evidence relating to 'Interaction' at the beginning of Key Stage 1.

Attitudes

This is not assessed formally through the National Curriculum but is a consideration for all teachers in assessing what it is that motivates the child or the difficulties they may be encountering. For instance, in English AT2 teachers will be analysing pupils' attitudes to books and reading, and considering whether they choose to read, whether they need to be encouraged, whether they appear to sit with a book for a reasonable period of time, and analysing the kinds of cues they are using. All of these attitudes are likely to be recorded in the *Classroom Observation Notebook* and transferred to the summative record.

Investigating/Problem-solving

There is a direct relationship between Maths AT1 (Using and Applying Maths) and English AT1. Strand 1 of the Maths curriculum is 'problem-solving', and strand 2 (reasoning, logic and proof) involves investigating and making predictions. The English AT1 as described above requires children to use talk for problem-solving. Similarly, skills of prediction, estimation and classifying permeate both Maths and Science. Strand 1 of Maths AT5 (collecting and processing) has a clear relationship with the 'PROCESS' heading 'Investigating/Problem-solving' which involves areas such as organising and classifying.

Communicating, representing and interpreting

The Maths AT5 (Handling Data) strand 2 (representing and interpreting) is not introduced until Level 3 – that is, for bright seven-year-olds. It is interesting to note that it is seen as an important aspect for observation within the 'PROCESS' system. It is possible that some very useful discussions might take place with parents and teacher colleagues at the end of Key Stage 1 when this area would only recently have been introduced through the National Curriculum but would nevertheless have been seen by the school as a central feature of the child's experience from an early age and would therefore have been commented upon at entry to Y1.

Needless to say, all of the English ATs relate directly to this element of the 'PROCESS' framework.

The Science AT1 (Scientific Investigation) contributes to 50 per cent of assessment at the end of Key Stage 1 and in fact permeates all areas of the 'PROCESS' headings. In strand 1 of this target the children are required to ask questions, predict and hypothesise, in strand 2 to observe, measure and manipulate variables and in strand 3 to interpret results and evaluate their scientific evidence. In AT2 (Life and Living Things), children will have had experience of strand 1 (life processes and the organisation of living things) by, for example, digging in the nursery/reception class garden, and this will have been recorded right across the 'PROCESS' headings.

REFERENCES

Department of Education and Science (1988) *DES Press Notice 175/88*, 7 June 1988.

Department of Education and Science/Welsh Office (1988) *National Curriculum: Task Group on Assessment and Testing: A report*. London: Department of Education and Science.

National Curriculum Council (1989) *A framework for the primary curriculum (Curriculum Guidance 1)*. York: National Curriculum Council.

Part Two

A framework of support

5

Introducing the 'PROCESS' system

In this chapter we describe the way in which 'PROCESS' was introduced to teachers and nursery nurses taking part in the piloting and evaluation project, and discuss questions which we feel need to be considered when introducing 'PROCESS' in classrooms, schools and LEAs. It should be borne in mind that this is intended as an account of our introductory INSET programme, and of teachers' response to it, and not necessarily as a blueprint for similar programmes elsewhere.

THE DAY SCHOOL

In the London Borough of Merton, where the 'PROCESS' materials were developed, a commitment was made to introduce the materials to each new cohort of schools by means of a full day's INSET. Accordingly, cover was arranged and financed (or in some cases a decision was made to close the nursery for the day) so that nursery teachers, nursery nurses and some members of ancillary staff could be released to attend a Day School at the Roehampton Institute. Over three years, three such days were provided as each new group of teachers entered the project.

Each Day School followed the same pattern:

Day School programme
9.00–10.15	Introductory session: 'PROCESS' purpose and rationale
10.15–10.45	Coffee
10.45–12.15	Workshops I
	Group A: *Classroom Observation Notebook*
	Group B: *Parent Discussion Record*
12.15–13.15	Lunch
13.15–14.45	Workshops II
	Group B: *Classroom Observation Notebook*
	Group A: *Parent Discussion Record*

14.45–15.15	Plenary session: Action planning; future meetings; sources of support
15.15–15.30	Tea and depart

Each of the three main sessions (Introductory session; Workshop on *Classroom Observation Notebook*; Workshop on *Parent Discussion Record*) are described in turn below.

INTRODUCTORY SESSION

Welcome and introduction and brief outline of the day

Introduction to the 'PROCESS' project: A short talk on the background to the project, the rationale and purpose behind the materials, general introduction to the elements of the package.

Introductory activity

- As individuals, write down what you are hoping to achieve by using 'PROCESS'.
- As a small group, compare aims and attempt to establish priorities.
- Feed back to whole group. Gather on overhead projector (OHP) or flipchart.
- These aims can be referred to later in the day and in subsequent sessions, to clarify priorities and to maintain resolve when the going gets tough!

WORKSHOP ON THE *CLASSROOM OBSERVATION NOTEBOOK*

This workshop closely follows Chapter 3.
Resources needed: Prepared OHP slides; blank OHP slides/flipchart and pens; video player; notebooks for dissemination.
Aims of the session:

- To take teachers through the section in the Guide about using the *Classroom Observation Notebook*, and to help them to think about options available to them.
- To explore the meanings of the terms used on the flap, by presentation, by using the notebook to record observations of a child featured on a video, and by discussion.

Introductory remarks

Acknowledge that finding time to observe and record is one of the most challenging aspects of teaching. Refer back to aims from introductory session, to remind teachers why it is worth making the effort. Emphasise that 'PROCESS' provides a flexible system, and teachers will have to make personal decisions about the details of the system that they decide to operate, as well as the amount of recorded observation that is manageable in their particular situation. Acknowledge that note-taking styles are inevitably personal and will vary with different people and the situations in which the observations occur.

It is important to strike a balance between providing a support and a straitjacket in all of this. If you are aware of the constraints and pressures that the particular group of teachers are working under, and of their experience of doing observations and record-keeping previously, you will be able to tailor your remarks accordingly. It is necessary to convey a clear structure of procedures and framework, and set some levels of use to aim for, otherwise teachers may feel confused and daunted by too many options. On the other hand, there must be some flexibility in the way 'PROCESS' is used, if numbers of children and staff, for instance, vary within the group. If procedures are too rigid, or unrealistically high goals are set, teachers will become despondent, or feel guilty that they are not doing it 'right'. As one teacher remarked, 'It's like Weightwatchers'! Of course she was referring to the need to make a commitment which, once done, made things seem easier. However, as with dieting, if people feel that they are failing, they may be tempted to give up altogether, or to feel inferior to others who seem to be on target. Providing support in setting realistic goals is addressed again in Chapter 6. Clarity, reassurance and acknowledgement of difficulties and room for personal differences in style, are the key ingredients here.

Presentation and use of the notebook

OHP1

USING THE *CLASSROOM OBSERVATION NOTEBOOK*

- The elements of the notebook

- Organising the notebook

- Making entries in the notebook

- Using the flap

Important points to cover (these are discussed in detail in Chapter 3):

- The notebook: reasons for its design features.
- Daily use: planned and incidental observations; 'story-fashion' or in boxes.
- The importance of commitment: identifying one's reasons for adopting the approach, and creating opportunities to be reminded of this.
- The importance of finding a personal style for making entries.

OHP2

PLANNING FOR OBSERVATION

- Organising the classroom

- Planning your time

- Promoting investigation and problem-solving in the classroom

---

Important points to cover (these are discussed in detail in Chapter 3):

- The importance of appropriate classroom resources, of encouraging self-reliance and of promoting group work and collaboration.
- Targeting: discuss options.
- Discuss alternative approaches to filing completed observation sheets.
- Introduce the notion of reviewing, and flag the summative stage – both for future discussions.

Discussion

Depending on time available, discuss in pairs or small groups the advantages of different options for deciding who to observe? when? where? and how many?

In our sessions, we have given people time to think about this over lunch, and come to some decisions at the end of the day, or alternatively when they got back to school and consulted with any absent colleagues. Since some people have considerable difficulty in getting started, especially if they have other problems, or too many decisions to make, you may want, at this point, to:

- provide one model for everybody, to try out and report back on their attempts;
- discuss advantages and disadvantages of various options; or
- identify possible problems with each approach as well as strategies for tackling these.

Alternatively, you might end the day with everyone making a commitment to a personalised action plan. What you decide will depend upon the homogeneity of the teachers in your group, whether colleagues have to be consulted back at school, and the level of support teachers are likely to receive within their institutions.

Discussion of the flap headings

OHP3

USING THE FLAP TO STRUCTURE OBSERVATIONS AND ENTRIES

- DATE, NAME, TIME and OCCASION

- INTERACTION
  - social context
  - social behaviour related to the context
  - range of social skills

- ATTITUDES
  - response to the context
  - dispositions and interests
  - curiosity and persistence

- INVESTIGATING/PROBLEM-SOLVING
  - seeing what would happen if . . .
  - predicting; estimating
  - children making, using and articulating their own rules
  - organising, sorting and classifying
  - making and spotting patterns (repeating sequences, symmetry)
  - generalising, making links between one context and another
  - choosing appropriate methods, materials or tools for a purpose

- **COMMUNICATING, REPRESENTING AND INTERPRETING**
  - talking and listening
  - writing and reading
  - using numerals, tallies, fingers
  - drawing and painting
  - dance, mime and gesture
  - role play, imaginative play and storying
  - construction models, maps, plans and diagrams

- **INDIVIDUAL NEEDS/S.E.N. COMMENTARY**
  - significance of this observation
  - concerns about the child
  - action to be taken

Go through the prompts with examples, inviting examples from the group. You may wish to give teachers a few minutes after each heading is introduced to discuss and provide their own examples. You will probably wish to provide your own anecdotal examples of behaviour, in particular that which might fall into two or more categories (such as communication and interaction), and also of behaviour which may appear not to fit any headings, such as counting or using scissors.

Video-based observation

In this part of the session we suggest that the group views a short extract of video showing young children engaged in everyday activity in a nursery or reception class, for the purpose of a simulated observation and entry in the notebook. We used the ILEA video 'Looking at Shape and Space' (Part 1 'The Nursery'), but any clip showing children in a real setting should work.
   We suggest the following steps for this activity:

- Ask the teachers to use the notebooks to make observations of one child while watching the tape, trying to relate the entry to the flap headings. Emphasise that it's important to describe what the child is doing, rather than making interpretations or judgements.
- Take a few minutes to allow teachers to complete their notes.
- Invite teachers to compare their entries with one other person.
- Discuss in fours, or with the whole group:

  - feelings about doing it;
  - how you did it ('boxing' or not);
  - what you noted; and
  - similarities, differences.

Note emerging comments/problems on OHP or flipchart.

- As a whole group, discuss the use you would make of this observation, allowing for the fact that the child is not known to anyone in the group. What action or planning would follow from this observation, and from the way the entry had been structured by the flap headings?
- Possible suggestions (these relate to the specific video we used):

  - support the child in a structured small group situation;
  - encourage the child to role play or talk about a book;
  - develop domestic interests (e.g. laying table);
  - develop washing-up interest by providing water;
  - develop organising interest by giving shop equipment and shelving, other tidying situations, collections of things to be sorted;
  - develop space-filling interest by giving trays with shapes, boxes and bags to fill;
  - develop shape interest by encouraging play with plastic shapes, playdough biscuits, construction.

- Emphasise that these suggestions will be about opportunities to observe in different contexts to find out more and test interpretations of interests etc., rather than prescriptions following a single categorical assessment of the child's behaviour.
- Finally, emphasise that different people will notice different things and interpret them differently, so all observations are necessarily tentative.

Equally we all use the notebooks in slightly different ways: there is no one right way to observe and make entries, and no single 'true' observation.

WORKSHOP ON THE *PARENT DISCUSSION RECORD*

Resources needed: Prepared OHP showing notebook flap; flipchart/ large sheets of paper/blank OHP transparencies/whiteboard and pens; video player and monitor; video recording of parent–teacher discussion (see note below).
Aims of the session:

- To provide a clear rationale for discussion with parents.
- To talk through the notes in the Guide on using the notebook.
- To talk through the 'Possible topics of conversation' on the flap.

Note on parent–teacher video

In order to show what this conversation might look like, and to demonstrate some approaches, a video recording was made of a conversation between a mother whose son was about to start in a nursery class and a 'teacher'. In fact, the mother was the Borough's Early Years Advisory Teacher and the 'teacher' was a member of the Roehampton Institute staff who had, until recently, been a teacher. It had been decided to make this role-play video because it was not felt appropriate to put one of the Borough's parents in the position of taking part in a public conversation about a real child. It was possible for the simulated discussion to be very realistic because the child being discussed was unknown to the 'teacher' and was actually about to start school. The decision to make such a recording was taken because there was no other material known to us which could demonstrate such an informal conversation. It was felt to be important that teachers should have a starting point for discussion and a context within which they could raise issues of concern. It was not intended that the video should be presented as a model of 'how to do it'; there were certainly many flaws and issues raised by the video. In particular, we were aware that this was a very 'middle-class' conversation between a white teacher and a white parent, and that it did not reflect the fact that many parents would, perhaps, prefer to talk in a language other than English.

Introductory remarks

Make reference to the considerable body of evidence about the value of close liaison with parents, and about the ways in which partnerships can be developed (see Chapter 2). Acknowledge the contribution that parents have made in the pre-school years and the need for teachers to draw on parents' knowledge about their children. Point out that a commitment to make strong links with parents needs to be made by the school as a whole – not just by individual teachers – and that time needs to be made available for teachers to meet with parents in this way.

Refer to the ways in which schools already make contact with parents. It can be useful, at this stage, to list on the flipchart or OHP the kinds of liaison already in place. These will probably include:

- parents and children visiting the classroom;
- meetings for parents explaining school procedures and expectations;
- visits to homes to talk about school, get to know children, take school booklets, etc.; and
- parents' evenings in school to show work and talk about progress.

Make the point that this kind of meeting is for schools and teachers to inform parents. Explain that the purpose of the 'PROCESS' parent discussion is to invite parents to inform teachers about their children, and to share their extensive knowledge, so that teachers can use that knowledge as a starting point in school. It is important to stress this distinction, since this sort of conversation with parents may be quite new to teachers.

Presentation of the notebook

Participants should have the opportunity to handle the notebooks. Point out the way in which the pages are organised and how the flap works (see Chapter 2). Talk about preparation for the conversation and the facility offered on the recording sheets for preparatory notes. Such notes might include topics of particular relevance to an individual parent or family, or observations of the child which could act as a starting point for the conversation. If possible, show preparatory jottings on an OHP transparency.

Present the headings from the flap on an OHP transparency.

Part one: introduction and explanation

Explain the importance of giving an informal introduction to the conversation, and of explaining to parents that the teacher hopes to listen to their account of the child and that it is not intended as an occasion for telling parents about the child (see notes in Chapter 2).

Part two: the conversation

Useful openers: Invite participants to suggest other possible ways of 'breaking the ice' in addition to those already suggested on the flap.

Possible topics of conversation: Make the point that these topics do not represent an agenda to be worked through. Stress the notion that this is intended to be a conversation, and that any number of other topics may arise as it goes on. Point out, too, that the order of topics is not significant, that some may need more time than others and that it is useful to have the flap open to refer to new topics if conversation dries up.

Talk through the list of topics, pointing out that the wording for each topic should be framed in a way that leads to natural conversation. Most headings are self-explanatory, though 'characteristic or noticeable things the child does whilst playing' has generally needed some explanation and examples (i.e. 'she sings to herself when she is concentrating' or 'he gives a running commentary when he is playing with model animals or building with bricks or Lego').

Emphasise that the issue of 'languages used at home' needs to be handled sensitively; suggest that by making a positive comment about how good it is for people to be able to use more than one language teachers will indicate that they value this ability. If there is time you could invite suggestions for other topics not included in this list.

Remind teachers that they will need to make brief notes during the conversation. Single words are often enough to make sure a point is not forgotten. If possible show an example of conversation jottings on an OHP transparency or flipchart.

At this point show the video recording of the parent/teacher conversation. Teachers can be invited to make jottings of the kind they might make for themselves, while they listen. They can also be asked to consider issues raised by this particular conversation. This should be followed by an opportunity for discussion, initially in groups of three or four. Groups can then bring to a plenary session the issues they have discussed. Points should be written up on flipchart, board or OHP.

After this activity, return to the OHP transparency of flap headings.

Part three: summing up

Make the point that this summary needs to be agreed by the parent(s) and that you should make clear what is being written down. The summary on the recording sheet can be completed immediately following the conversation so that parent(s) can see it there and then. Some teachers prefer to write up the summary later and then show it to parent(s) at a further meeting or informal encounter. Either way is perfectly acceptable: what is important is that parents should have the opportunity to see and comment upon what has been recorded.

Finally, emphasise that undertaking this kind of discussion with parents requires careful planning. Thought needs to be given to:

- the value of such meetings: why should you do it;
- how invitations should be given;
- the space to be used for meeting parents;
- who will meet which parents;

- cover for teachers to create time for meetings;
- whole-school commitment; and
- translation/interpreting requirements.

QUESTIONS TO CONSIDER WHEN INTRODUCING 'PROCESS'

In our experience, the decision to introduce the 'PROCESS' system requires consideration of a number of critical issues. We list below the kinds of questions which we observed teachers, schools, 'early years groups' and local authorities addressing in advance of the practical implementation of the package.

QUESTIONS TO BE CONSIDERED BY THE CLASS TEACHER

There will already be a system of recording and assessment in place and a form of classroom organisation in operation. 'PROCESS' only works success-fully in a classroom where there is a willingness to experiment with forms of provision which promote children's autonomy and where observation is regarded as an integral aspect of teaching and learning.

Recording and assessing

- What will the system offer me that others do not?
- How will I organise my time so that I am able to make provision for conversations with parents?
- What training or support will I receive for my conversations with parents?
- Will I be able to make notes and talk at the same time?
- What shall I do if the parents don't say much?
- What will I do if both parents come and they don't agree with each other?
- Can I observe and interact with the children at the same time?
- Will I still have to complete other record-keeping systems?
- When shall I do all the writing for the summative record?
- How many entries will I need for each child?
- How will I know if I have a sufficient variety of observations?
- How will I find time to talk to the parents about the summative record?
- Could it serve a similar function to the annual report to parents?
- How will I pass/discuss the information to/with the next teacher?
- I'm not sure if I should write in the 'Next steps' box because the receiving teacher might not agree with me. Should I talk to the next teacher first?

Classroom organisation and management

- If I'm the only teacher who is interested how can I implement this system on my own?
- I know that observing children is a good idea but when I tried it before I never managed to have my notebook or pen to hand.
- What will I do if another child wants me or there is a problem in the home corner?
- How will the children know that I can't be interrupted?
- Is my organisation good enough for this project?
- Can my children work on their own?
- What kind of activities do I provide?
- Are they interesting activities which encourage the children to talk and investigate?
- How and when should I ask for the support and help of my headteacher?
- How will I know if this system is working well?

QUESTIONS TO BE CONSIDERED BY THE SCHOOL

If the senior management team is committed to the introduction of 'PROCESS' then there is a fair chance that it will be successful, but commitment by all the staff must be agreed. Imposition is unsatisfactory.

- How should the senior management team set about introducing this system to the staff?
- How shall we reach agreement that this is a good approach?
- How does this system sit with our rationale for learning and teaching?
- What are the implications for classroom management and organisation?
- How does it dovetail with the school system?
- How should we integrate with other staff/helpers, e.g. bi-lingual support teachers/assistants, parents?
- How will we manage time for parent conversations during the day?
- If additional support is given to nursery and reception teachers for parent conversations how will the other teachers react?
- How will teachers respond to yet another initiative?
- Will it be necessary to dispense with previous systems for recording?
- Will this system provide enough information about children's achievements at point of entry to Y1?
- Will teachers accept it as reliable and valid evidence of children's achievements?
- Will the receiving teacher know how to continue with the child?
- Will we need to set up a system of evaluation?
- What INSET will we need to consider outside of learning about the project itself, e.g. child development, observation techniques?
- How shall we organise for information to be passed on from nursery to reception/receiving teachers?

QUESTIONS TO BE CONSIDERED BY THE 'EARLY YEARS GROUP'

It is possible that a group of early years co-ordinators may be interested in introducing 'PROCESS' into their schools where rather traditional systems of assessing children are in place.

- Our schools have systems in place already. How will this be incorporated into the schools' systems for record-keeping and assessment?
- How can we convince our heads that this is worth trying?
- Are there any members of staff who would be interested in working with us?
- Will receiving teachers accept this as valid and reliable evidence of children's achievements?
- How can we transmit our enthusiasm to all the staff?
- We can't expect teachers to continue with a dual system so we must have support and agreement that we use only one system. How can we mobilise this?
- How do we ensure that this receives a high profile in the schools?

QUESTIONS TO BE CONSIDERED BY THE LOCAL EDUCATION AUTHORITY

Some LEAs have encouraged schools to devise their own assessment systems so a number of issues would need to be considered.

- Why do we wish to promote 'PROCESS'?
- Do we envisage that this will replace previous assessment systems?
- Will this become known as the LEA Early Years Assessment System?
- Is the funding available to offer training for teachers?
- What will be the structure for training?
- Are we asking schools to provide their own funding?
- Is this to be adopted for all nursery and reception classes?
- Will this system be piloted with a small group of schools first? If so, should these schools be nominated or invitations sent to all schools?
- How will this be incorporated with systems of assessment in KS1 and KS2?
- Will it offer receiving teachers the kind of information they think they will need to inform their planning for the National Curriculum?
- Will it provide a baseline of assessment which can be used with National Curriculum assessment results at the end of Key Stage 1?
- Who will be the target groups for training: nursery nurses/nursery teachers/reception teachers?
- Should we target headteachers separately for awareness-raising and training?
- Should it be phased in over a period of time?
- How shall the system be introduced?

- How will they react to the implementation of a system which initially seems to demand more time?
- How much time can be devoted to this project by the Inspectorate and the Advisory Teachers?
- How will we monitor and evaluate the implementation of this project?

6

Reviewing 'PROCESS'

In this chapter we describe the forms of support we offered to teachers taking part in the 'PROCESS' project, and conclude by summarising the lessons we learned as a result of our pilot work.

'TWILIGHT' SESSIONS

Following the initial Day School to introduce 'PROCESS' (see Chapter 5), we held regular 'twilight' sessions at the professional development centre throughout the year for teachers taking part in the project. These were of two types. The first type were related specifically to features of the 'PROCESS' system, and were designed to be support sessions for teachers new to the project, involving feedback from individuals, exchange of ideas, and general encouragement to all concerned. We refer to these below as 'INSET sessions'.

The second type concentrated on more general aspects of practice and provision in the early years classroom. These sessions, which we refer to below as 'input sessions', were offered to teachers taking part in the pilot in direct response to their request for opportunities to explore alternatives to conventional approaches to the organisation of teaching and learning. Teachers attempting to integrate the 'PROCESS' materials into their everyday routine quickly discovered that changes to their approach were required in order to ensure the successful development of what we describe in Chapter 1 as 'observation-led teaching'. In this sense teachers recognised that the 'PROCESS' material could be used not only to record children's behaviour but also as a system for evaluating and changing their own practice. As a result, the project team offered input sessions on imaginative play, block play and early literacy. Each of these input sessions explored the place of a specific area in the early years curriculum, and showed how valuable 'PROCESS' could be in evaluating practice and provision as well as providing valuable evidence of children's competence in different areas.

We describe below some of the INSET sessions and input sessions we ran during the development phase of the 'PROCESS' project. These are presented in the form of notes addressed to potential INSET providers for you to select and use as appropriate.

INSET SESSIONS

We found that although teachers left the Day School inspired to start, some teachers had not managed to make a start by the time of the first twilight meeting. The twilight sessions therefore played a vital role in rekindling the enthusiasm and determination to move forward. Hearing from colleagues who had made a start on their observations, and listening to some of the very positive comments they made about how they were beginning to see children in different lights (having seen them operate in previously unnoticed areas), provided a much needed stimulus to others. The feedback comments gave a 'realness' to the value of 'PROCESS' which inspired some of the more hesitant to make a more determined start when they returned to school.

Session 1 – Managing observations

This session should take place shortly after the initial Day School, with the date clearly identified beforehand.
Aims of the session:

- To help maintain momentum in observation and parent discussion.
- To encourage people to start making observations.
- To deepen understanding of the rationale behind 'PROCESS'.

(a) Who has made a start?

A general question is needed to ascertain how many have made a start. If some have made a start it is easy then to explore their ways of operating before looking at problems in starting that others have experienced.

(b) How did they go about this?

List strategies on OHP/whiteboard/flipchart, etc. Possible strategies which might be fed back:

- Talking to head
- Talking to staff meeting
- Involving other nursery/reception staff
- Putting sheets in strategic places
- Giving each member of team own notebook
- Targeting children

(c) What are the benefits?

List some of the benefits that the teachers already feel they are gaining from their initial observations, e.g. seeing children in different contexts than normal, seeing different patterns to a child's interaction, understanding, behaviour, etc.

(d) What problems have others had getting started?

If these are invited in an unjudgemental and unthreatening way they can provide a useful focus for discussion. Can they be grouped in any way? Possible categories include the following:

- Whole-school problems
- Classroom organisation
- People
- Time
- Observations

(e) How can/have people overcome these problems?

Some of the strategies identified in response to (b) might provide starting points for discussion. Ask groups to formulate lists of possible strategies. Share as a large group.

Possible suggestions:

- Whole school
    - talk to headteacher about 'PROCESS' and its purpose
    - address a staff meeting
    - talk to headteacher about time for parent discussions
- Classroom organisation
    - organising resources differently
    - strategies to encourage independence
    - place notebooks or clipboards in strategic places
- People
    - involve all staff in 'PROCESS'
    - encourage them to attend INSET if practical
    - provide equal access to notebooks
    - sharing ideas
    - strategies to remember to do observations, e.g. notice, planning time together
- Time
    - share tasks more to free someone to observe
    - plan observation time into daily/weekly schedule
    - build sharing time into schedule
    - prioritise observations, e.g. older children, those causing concern

- Observations
    - what to write
    - how to write – 'boxing' and 'not boxing'
    - setting the context
    - what is 'objectivity' in an activity such as this?

(f) Developing action plans

Ask people to work in school groups or area clusters to develop an action plan for the next stage. Encourage groups to set realistic and achievable goals. These do not necessarily have to be shared with the larger group.

(g) Plenary session

This short session should be used to encourage people so that they leave re-energised in the value of 'PROCESS' and determined to start or continue with their observations and parent discussions.

(h) Review sheets (reproduced in 'Reviewing observations' in Chapter 3)

Give these out for teachers to record where, when and how many observations they are making. To be brought to the next twilight session in two to three weeks.

Session 2 – Reviewing observations

This session can be separate or combined with the first session. It should take place as the number of observations is gradually increasing and asks teachers to consider some of the more practical aspects of 'PROCESS' as well as some of the underlying fundamentals.
Aims of the session:

- To explore ways of storing observations.
- To review the nature of observations made.
- To reflect on the implications for the classroom of such observations.

(a) What use have you made of the review sheet?

Collect together comments made by group on OHP or flipchart. Possible examples may include some or all of the following:

- Seen a previously unidentified pattern in a child's behaviour
- Seen friendship patterns not seen before
- Realised children 'missing' from observations
- Identified areas not observed
- Some activities do not lend themselves to useful observations

(b) What kinds of action have you taken as a result of recording observations?

Have you altered your provision in any way? Some possible comments at this stage might include:

- Re-site some provision
- Keep some provision there on a more permanent basis
- Provide more and different equipment in particular areas
- Change way observations are planned to cover all or more areas
- Development of alternative review sheets to track children

(c) What kinds of observation can be made?

This question follows on naturally from the above discussion and actually allows one to explore in some detail different kinds of observations.

In groups discuss the possible kinds of observation that could be set up. For example:

- Mapping areas: Observing an area of provision and mapping the use over a period of time will give you an insight into whether or not it is well-used and provides the challenges and experiences you had anticipated. It will also identify those children who do or do not visit that area.
- Tracking a child to identify strengths and interests or because of concerns: A video made in a local nursery was used to show how tracking a child enabled one to see patterns and interests in the child's mind. There are many videos available commercially that have extracts that can be used in this way and it is possible to make your own to support this section.
- Incidental observations: Pick one or two incidental observations. What did you note? What made you pick these? What did you do as a result? They may have been picked because they gave new insights to an individual such as knowledge exhibited, new friendships, good communication skills, good manipulative and social skills, great imagination and/or initiative, etc.
- Planned area observations: In observing a particular area it is possible to identify children who never visit that area or those who stay there for most of the session. Look at the way children use the area – possibilities for supporting and extending children's ideas/activities.

(d) What makes a good situation for an observation?

Video material is available that will enable you to have the whole group observing a child and then to feed back their findings. We used the video from the Open University's study pack *Working with the under-fives* – in particular, an excerpt where Helen is playing in the café. This was viewed by the group and observations were shared and compared with the OU's notes. A remarkable degree of accord is shown among teachers when they do this exercise and it is very supportive and reassuring for them to realise that they focus on similar key events.

Ask the group to consider what makes for good provision for observing. Ideas might include:

- A good basic provision
- A wide range of basic areas always available
- Presenting unusual materials
- Posing problems
- Challenging interaction by adults in role
- Using parent discussion to inform provision
- Setting up co-operative tasks and play

Certain activities where children are engaged in practice or routine tasks do not generally provide the observations that allow us to see the cognitive elements that are listed on the flap. These latter kinds of tasks will give a picture of the child's physical and manipulative skills. The essential point here is that 'PROCESS' offers the chance to build a wider but qualitative picture of a child and therefore enables us to provide a richer environment for all.

Session 3 – Storing entries

This was a group discussion to explore how teachers store completed recording sheets in the short and long term. In the short term observations are collected together in some way, often left in file or folder and then a review is carried out at regular intervals when they are filed more systematically.

Long-term possibilities include filing observations:

- chronologically by date of observation;
- under child's name; or
- in child's profile or portfolio.

The link between 'PROCESS' and other school recording and assessment schemes is a point that arises at this stage, and is an on-going development in most schools. This is an opportunity to discuss the place of 'PROCESS' within the school's schemes, as well as the purposes of record-keeping and reporting, and is extremely valuable in extending people's ideas for records throughout the school. The storage of the recording sheets from parent discussions raises similar points and also adds to the debate about the purpose of records.

Session 4 – Discussions with parents

Resources needed: Large sheets of paper and felt-tip pens; flipchart/
whiteboard and pens.
Aims of the session:

- To review progress in arranging parent discussions.
- To discuss issues raised after initial discussions have been held.
- To share strategies for overcoming some of the problems that have
  arisen.

Introductory activity

Teachers work in groups with large sheets of paper. The discussion is
divided into two parts:

- Why we would want to talk with parents and advantages of doing
  so.
- Factors preventing us from doing so.

In groups discuss and list views under each heading.

Each group contributes the one point they feel to be most important to
composite lists written on flipchart by session leader.

A list of advantages will remind teachers why they thought parent
discussions were worth undertaking. Sessions produced the following
points:

- Valuing the parents' knowledge and expertise, creating mutual respect
- Developing relationships begun in pre-school home visits
- Starting a positive relationship between school and parents
- Building a relationship with the parents
- Gathering information to use as a starting point in the classroom
- Finding out important information about children's interests and
  building a more rounded picture of each child
- Giving parents the opportunity to voice any concerns or worries
- Getting to know parents who seem less communicative or are not
  often seen in school

The question of factors preventing parent discussions happening was
then opened for discussion to enable teachers to offer possible supportive
solutions. The following are some of issues identified:

(a) Time

How can time be made to talk to parents in the school day?

This was a particular issue in reception classes where there was no
ancillary support. In nursery classes there was more flexibility because of
the nursery nurse support.

Some suggested solutions:

- Get a whole-school commitment to becoming involved in discussions with parents, so that use can be made of support from colleagues in the school (e.g. headteacher, part-time teachers) to enable class teachers to be released to meet parents.
- Use time at the beginning and end of the day and be willing to be flexible in accommodating families' needs by carrying out some discussions in the evening.
- Give up the formal 'parents' evening' and use the time for individual conversations.
- Start the term or half-term a day later and use that time either for home visits or in-school appointments.

(b) Space

Where there is no parents' room, how can an informal relaxed place be created?

Some suggested solutions:

- Use the headteacher's room, but ensure that both parties in the conversation are seated in easy chairs, rather than the teacher behind the desk, and make certain there will be no interruptions (e.g. telephone, children, visitors).
- Create a screened area in a corridor, with easy chairs, where there is not likely to be constant traffic.
- Use a part of the staff room at times other than break/lunch.
- Use the classroom during assembly or while the children are involved in activities outside the room.

(c) Parents not fluent in English

How can conversations be held when there is no community language support teacher available in the school?

Some suggested solutions:

- Ensure that invitations to school are made in the first language of the home and that an explanation is offered of the purpose of the discussion. This may mean getting a written invitation translated rather than inviting orally.
- Suggest that another family member or friend who speaks English more fluently comes along to the discussion. This is preferable to using an interpreter who does not know the family context, though this service might be offered if there is no alternative.

(d) Parents unable/unwilling to come to school during school hours

How can contact be made with parents who 'never come to school'?
Some suggested solutions:

- Consider whether invitations make it possible for both parents to attend together, where this is appropriate. One person may feel anxious about coming to school. If possible allow parents to suggest a convenient time.
- Consider whether there are younger children who cannot be left alone and whether the offer of crêche/minding facilities would help.
- Offer a home visit, if there appear to be insurmountable difficulties.

(e) Where to start when there are large numbers

When there are 50 children (25 morning and 25 afternoon) in the nursery, how can teachers talk to all of the parents?
Some suggested solutions:

- Devise a rolling programme – it is unlikely that all of these will be starting at the same time.
- Start with those who are to transfer to another class the soonest and work back towards the youngest.
- Start with the new entrants and build up the programme gradually (this may mean not holding discussions with the parents of children already established in the nursery unless there are pressing reasons to do so).
- In reception classes spread the discussions over the first term or, if there is a staggered entry, the first few weeks of each term.
- Spread the load between members of staff – in a large Early Years Unit there are likely to be several members of staff, so that everyone, including nursery nurses, could be involved in meeting with parents.

INPUT SESSIONS

As explained at the beginning of this chapter, these sessions were developed in response to requests from teachers taking part in the pilot project for opportunities to explore methods of organising teaching and learning in the early years classroom so that observation could become an integral part of practice. Three 'input sessions' were offered, in the areas of imaginative play, block play and early literacy.

Session 1 – Imaginative play

Aims of the session:

- To explore the role of 'PROCESS' in developing the provision for imaginative play.

- To explore the role of the teacher in imaginative play through use of 'PROCESS'.

The group was asked to bring some observations of imaginative play with them and to choose one 'good' one.

Groups were asked to identify the themes that recur. These themes were collated onto an OHP.

The themes could be wide-reaching but nearly always included some or all of the following:

Averted threat	Taking a trip
Telephoning	Shopping
Packing	Cooking
Eating	Treating/healing
Building/repairing	

We then addressed the question, 'What is significant about imaginative play of this kind?' Some elements of play that can be identified by close observation, according to research quoted by Smith (1988), include:

- Ability to get in and out of the action
- Length of time in the activity
- 'Patterners' explore properties/use of objects
- 'Dramatisers' imagine non-present objects, events and persons
- Transformations – symbolic use of non-structured materials
- Complexity of play – variety of activities; concepts; communication; number of characters

We then examined each of the four substantive headings on the flap of the *Classroom Observation Notebook* to see how they might be used to structure observations of imaginative play.

(a) Interaction

- How have they interacted? Who with?
- Social context: do they follow social norms?
- Pretending, e.g. turning on taps, putting water in, making tea/cakes, dressing up
- Imitating real life

(b) Attitudes

- What perseverance, persistence, co-operation, etc. do they exhibit? Evidence?
- Caring for others
- Concentration

(c) Investigating/Problem-solving

- Do they use 'what if' questions?
- Do they organise, sort, make patterns, repeat sequences, choose appropriate tools and resources, modify and adapt work patterns?
- Do they make up rules?
- Is the play repetitive?

(d) Communicating, Representing and Interpreting

- Do they listen and respond to each other?
- Do they write, read, draw, paint, mime, gesture, role play, imaginatively play or 'story'?
- Do they model in some form?

Report back on the examples the teachers have chosen. Have they other observations to add to the pattern or challenge it? Do they need to look for similar observations in other areas or contexts? Do they need to develop interaction strategies to extend the play or to investigate depth of under-standing seen? Six essential elements for teachers to work on for play are identified by Smith (1988). These are:

- Interaction with play partners
- Persistence in play episodes
- Imitative play
- Make-believe in regard to objects
- Make-believe in regard to actions and situations
- Verbal communication related to play episode

When play involves all these elements, adult intervention might be phased out. Direct intervention is not appropriate for children engaged in high-quality socio-dramatic play.

The session closed with a review of the ways in which promoting play of this kind (a) enables important kinds of learning, (b) frees the teacher to adopt an observing role, and (c) produces evidence for recording.

Session 2 – Block play

Aims of the session:

- To examine construction provision in the nursery.
- To explore its potential for investigations.
- To relate observations of block play to the headings on the flap.

(a) Introduction

A selection of block construction kits needs to be available for teachers to examine and answer the question 'What makes a good construction resource?'. Groups feed back their ideas after spending some time exploring the range of resources available.

(b) Feedback

Good provision might include:

- Having a wide range always available
- Kits that will blend together
- Kits that operate in different ways
- Presenting them to children in interesting ways, e.g. arranging kit in attractive form
- Presenting them to children as high status tasks
- Blending them with other materials such as wood, plastics, recyclable material
- Positive interaction
- Exploring ways to extend and support children with their work
- Posing problems to the children to stimulate inquiry, support and extend play

(c) Relating observations to the flap

An A3 sheet with the headings from the flap is given to the group. Groups suggest observations of children engaged in block play where the focus of the activity matches the categories on the flap. This enables teachers to explore the range of potential in construction activities. At the same time it allows them to explore and understand the headings in more depth. The use of real examples and the discussion that arises from these are very powerful instruments in the teachers' understanding.

(d) What constitutes progress in construction play?

Groups are asked now to try to identify evidence that would help to show progress in construction play. The real examples from which the course provider may have to work generally allow exploration of issues such as:

- Involvement
- Interaction whilst working
- Detail in construction
- Blending of kits
- Ability to join parts and other kits together
- Relationship with flap headings
- Exploration of mathematics and design technology

(e) Strategies for moving children on

Groups were asked to consider how to provide opportunities for extending children's competence. The suggestions fall into the same categories as already listed but the change in emphasis relates to selecting appropriate provision.

Slides from the Froebel Block Play Research Project (Gura, 1992) were used to explore potential and progression. The session closed with a review of the ways in which promoting play of this kind (a) enables important kinds of learning, (b) frees the teacher to adopt an observing role, and (c) produces evidence for recording.

Session 3 – Early literacy

Aim of the session:

● To provide some background information about children's early writing and common patterns of development, using examples which could form the basis of observation.

The session began with a survey of some of the research into young children's early writing. We reviewed the evidence that this begins long before children enter school. Much evidence exists that children's encounters with literacy at home and in the world at large develop their understandings about the purposes and functions of written language. Many children demonstrate a clear intention to convey meaning in their 'writing' long before they produce recognisable letter forms.

Reference was made to the work of Glenda Bissex (1980), Marie Clay (1975), Emilia Ferreiro and Anna Teberosky (1982), Shirley Payton (1984) and the National Writing Project (1990).

Examples were provided from this work and from classrooms, together with information about the context in which the 'writing' had been produced. Examples included:

● A list of questions
● A letter
● A story
● A song, with the clapping represented by stars
● A map of where the child's bedroom is situated in her house
● A telephone list, with 'numbers' and 'initials'
● A birthday card

The teachers were invited to comment on what each example revealed about that child's current hypotheses and understandings.

It was found that appropriate observations were made under several headings on the flap:

INTERACTION:

- When the child had collaborated with another in producing the 'writing', for example in role play.
- When the child had talked about the 'writing' either to an adult or to another child.

ATTITUDES:

- When the child had approached the task confidently.
- When the child had shown curiosity, had asked about the letters, had said 'what does it say?'.
- When the child showed persistence and concentration in the effort of recording the message.
- When this example reflected a particular interest in writing.

COMMUNICATING, REPRESENTING AND INTERPRETING:

- All examples of 'writing' needed some comment under this heading, perhaps about the child's intentions or understanding of written communication. Sometimes a comment might be made about the child's chosen mode of representation, e.g. letter-like shapes, pictures, letters, numerals, diagram or map, invented symbols and invented spellings.

We concluded this session by discussing the value of collecting examples of children's early 'writing' with comment under the flap headings. Observations recorded in this way provide a cumulative profile of development, with each 'snapshot' adding another piece to the whole picture. Comment was also made about the value of such examples in demonstrating progress to parents and about the way in which parents became aware of 'writing' that had been done at home, and added their own examples.

CONCLUDING REMARKS

CONDITIONS FOR THE SUCCESSFUL IMPLEMENTATION OF THE 'PROCESS' SYSTEM

At the time of preparing this Guide, the project team had piloted the 'PROCESS' material with three cohorts of schools, and had monitored and evaluated the progress of the project in those schools which had two or three years' experience of using the package. On the basis of this work we now feel able to summarise the factors which ensured the successful implementation of the 'PROCESS' system. In schools where the project was most effectively developed and sustained:

- there was an understanding by the whole staff of the value and place of 'PROCESS' within the school's system of record-keeping;
- observation was seen as an integral part of teaching and learning and was used to plan the next steps in the child's learning;
- value was given by the headteacher and classroom teachers to the participation of nursery nurses in the 'PROCESS' project;
- encouragement and praise were given to participating staff by the headteacher/member of the senior management team;
- 'PROCESS' was given a high profile through recognition in staff meetings, notices, newsletters, parent and governor meetings;
- teachers were encouraged to start with a realistic number of observations;
- the summative record was discussed with parents in a planned and coherent way;
- a reasonable amount of time for parent conferences was formally allocated;
- comfortable space was arranged for parent conferences; and
- time was set aside for nursery and reception teachers to discuss the summative record with receiving/Year 1 teachers.

REFERENCES

Bissex, Glenda (1980) *GYNS AT WRK*. Cambridge, Mass.: Harvard University Press.

Clay, Marie (1975) *What did I write?* London: Heinemann Educational Press.

Ferreiro, Emilia and Teberosky, Anna (1982) *Literacy before schooling*. London: Heinemann Educational Press.

Gura, P. (ed.) (1992) *Exploring learning: young children and block play*. London: Paul Chapman Publishing. (Information on booklet–slide package available from Tina Bruce, Roehampton Institute, Froebel Institute College, Grove House, Roehampton Lane, London SW15 5PJ.)

National Writing Project (1990) *Becoming a writer*. London: Thomas Nelson.

Open University (1990) *Working with under-fives*. Open University Study Pack PE635. Milton Keynes: Open University.

Payton, Shirley (1984) 'Developing awareness of print' in *Educational Review*.

Smith, P.K. (1988) 'The relevance of fantasy play for development in young children' in A. Cohen and L. Cohen (eds) *Early education: the preschool years*. London: Paul Chapman Publishing.

PROFILING, RECORDING AND OBSERVING

This Teachers' Guide is part of the PROFILING, RECORDING AND OBSERVING package which also includes two sturdy ringbound notebooks, the *Classroom Observation Notebook* and the *Parent Discussion Record* in which to record your observations.

Why not order a complete set for your school today?

PROFILING, RECORDING AND OBSERVING, Barry Stierer, Jane Devereux, Sue Gifford, Elizabeth Laycock and Janet Yerbury
Full set (2 notebooks plus teachers guide) 0-415-08966-2
Notebooks also available separately 0-415-08965-4

Available from all good bookshops. In case of difficulty or for further information, contact Routledge Customer services, ITPS, Cheriton House, North Way, Andover, Hants SP10 5BE Telephone 0264 332424.